Dear

Go for it!

Dangerously
ALIVE

Dangerously ALIVE

African adventures of faith under fire

Simon Guillebaud

MONARCH
BOOKS

Oxford, UK & Grand Rapids, Michigan, USA

First published in the UK in 2011 by Monarch Books
(a publishing imprint of Lion Hudson plc)
Wilkinson House, Jordan Hill Road, Oxford OX2 8DR, England
Tel: +44 (0)1865 302750 Fax: +44 (0)1865 302757
Email: monarch@lionhudson.com
www.lionhudson.com

Reprinted 2011

ISBN 978 0 85721 011 1 (print)
ISBN 978 0 85721 088 3 (epub)
ISBN 978 0 85721 087 6 (Kindle)
ISBN 978 0 85721 089 0 (PDF)

Distributed by:
UK: Marston Book Services, PO Box 269, Abingdon, Oxon, OX14 4YN
USA: Kregel Publications, PO Box 2607, Grand Rapids, Michigan 49501

British Library Cataloguing Data
A catalogue record for this book is available from the British Library.

Printed and bound in Great Britain by Clays Ltd, St Ives plc.

TO ALL THE MEMBERS OF THE
WORLDWIDE COMMUNITY THAT
MAKES UP ALLNATIONS – STUDENTS
AND STAFF, PAST AND PRESENT –
SCATTERED TO THE FOUR CORNERS
OF THE EARTH AND ENACTING JESUS'
CALL TO BE DANGEROUSLY ALIVE.

For more information, visit
www.allnations.ac.uk

CONTENTS

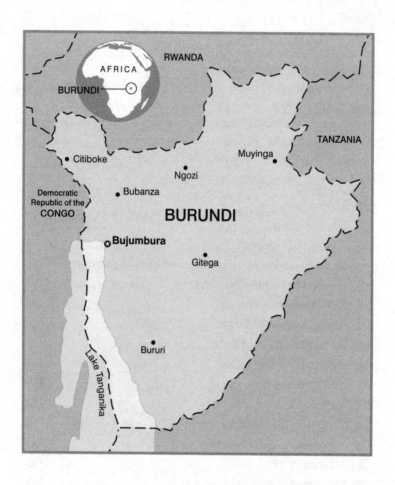

I sped around the bend in the road on my motorbike, but quickly scrambled to a stop, surprised to see a figure in the middle of the road, just ahead of me. He was holding a grenade in his hand, ready to blow me up. I knew this for a fact – he had made his intentions clear two days before when he'd written saying he was going to cut out my eyes.

I'd had some sleepless nights over the threat, of course, but I'd gone to stay at someone else's place for a while and was varying my routes around town so that he wouldn't know where to lie in wait for me.

My guard waved at me – a pre-arranged sign not to approach. This was both surreal and yet chillingly real.

"God, what on earth shall I do? If it has to be, I'm ready to die. Let's go…"

FOREWORD

What you have in front of you is a truly remarkable story. It is a tale of one man's determined obedience to his amazing God. If you allow it, this book will touch you, challenge you and change you.

In 1999, a few of us were on the beach by Lake Tanganyika just outside the capital of Burundi, Bujumbura. Simon was feeling a bit jaded and went off for a prayer-walk. He returned ten minutes later, looking refreshed and renewed. I asked him about his walk and he replied: "If God is worth anything, then He is worth everything."

That, in a nutshell, is the message of Simon Guillebaud's life. It is the message of his hundreds of preaches, of his prayer emails, of his *More Than Conquerors* book and DVD, and now of this book as well. It is a message that, as you will read, he has lived closer than most.

His journey takes us through more than a decade of living, working, struggling and persevering in one of the world's most challenging, dangerous and sapping environments. Through it all we see Simon time and again consider his options, weigh up decisions, and choose to give his trust, talents, and energies to Jesus; for He is worth all we can give Him.

I first met Simon a few months after he had arrived in Burundi. With his cheeky grin, assured presence and knobbly knees flashing as he pedaled his bike, we struck up an instant friendship. We bonded through a shared love of sport, a Christmas party playing with street kids, an evening spent huddled in a corridor as bullets flew overhead, a time when grenades exploded as we rode by, a period when we witnessed one third of the capital being forced into displacement camps a few miles from us – and much more. I had the privilege of seeing some of his first year up close. I saw him preach, met his colleagues and, as you will read, had the honor of being there to offer him supportive counsel after he experienced a nasty death threat.

I later returned in 2007 for a short visit. By then we were both married and had one child each. What amazed me was to remember back to that first time. I had met a young man with just a borrowed push-bike to his name. Now I was astonished to see the range and depth of the kingdom work being done: everything from a conference hall nearly complete, an orphanage, an AIDS project, a few schools, and through several local groups, a whole movement of young leaders, evangelists and disciples being equipped and empowered to transform the nation – hundreds of thousands of lives were being impacted. At times it can be quite hard to believe all we read, but I have been there; and trust me, these events are even more inspiring if you encounter them in person – a sure testimony to one man's determined obedience and, much more importantly, to his amazing God.

So fasten your seat belts, and be prepared for a breath-taking, jaw-dropping and tear-jerking ride. Drink deeply of the stories you read, and as you do so, allow your heart to be encouraged, inspired, challenged, and renewed. And may we similarly choose to give God our all!

Ed Walker

Tearfund's Disaster Management Team; author of *Reflections from the Scorched Earth*; Founder of Hope into Action (www.hopeintoaction.org.uk)

PROLOGUE

If you were to hear the word "Burundi", what would it mean to you? A random survey of people might produce some interesting results – ranging from those for whom it might as well be a brand of cheese, to those who have an inkling that it's a country, but are not quite sure where it's located and don't know much about it.

I have discovered that the majority of well-educated people – who would claim a degree of global awareness – know very little about this place.

So what is Burundi?

In brief, it is a beautiful, land-locked country in the heart of Africa. It doesn't have any oil, diamonds or other mineral deposits that might give it geopolitical significance, and so it remains one of the most forgotten countries in the world. It is a land of great suffering that has endured many years of civil war; a place where hideous atrocities have been perpetrated. Hundreds of thousands of its people have been killed. Rape and pillage have been commonplace. Life expectancy is in the forties and decreasing. AIDS is on the rise. Famines strike regularly in different provinces. Deforestation is preparing to slip the noose over the head of future generations, and over-population gets worse by the day due to the explosive birth rate. It is a place of great darkness.

Yet, in the darkest places, the light shines brightest. Despite all the grim statistics and stories, God's bigger story continues to be played out in the lives of an ever-increasing number of people. These people have been lied to, deceived, promised much and ultimately let down, but have still experienced for themselves the undeniable reality of God's powerful, personal intervention in their lives.

If you had never heard of Burundi before today or, like many, had only a vague idea that it is a country somewhere in Africa but not much more, well, I want you to know about it. Why? Because Burundi is host to some of the most amazing people on the planet – people whose stories deserve to be told. For the last decade I have had the pleasure (or perhaps "painful privilege" is a better description) of journeying alongside them – men and women whose faith has been so refined in the crucible of suffering as to produce beautiful gems, sparkling with the reflected light of their Maker. I want to share some of that journey with you.

My time spent in Burundi has been an adventure and frequently a dangerous one at that. At one time it was statistically the most dangerous nation in the world. Mine has been a journey full of tears and laughter, great highs and terrible lows, incredible successes and crushing failures, sapping despair and outrageous hope, miracles and tragedies, elation, frustration, corruption and deception... and the list could go on.

In the coming pages I have tried to recount with utmost frankness and honesty some of what has happened over the last decade, largely by sharing with you my prayer letters and diary entries. They provide snapshots of what it is like to live for Christ in a very different environment, and include reflections on life, death, the rise of Islam, encounters with witch doctors, marital tensions, outrage at injustice, exposing corruption, sexual temptation, cultural *faux pas* and much more. These snapshots have been edited in the interests of both brevity and political sensitivity. Where appropriate, names have been changed to protect identities.

I pray that the following pages are an encouragement to you in your own journey, a challenge to your faith, and an invitation you embrace to become *dangerously alive*.

Simon Guillebaud
February 2011

1

THE CALL

Calling is the truth that God calls us to Himself so decisively
that everything we are, everything we do, everything we have
is invested with a special devotion and dynamism lived out as a
response to His summons and service.

Os Guinness

It was August 1998 and I had recently finished living in the
East End of London whilst attending Bible College. For the
last year my constant prayer had been, "God, I trust you. I'll
do anything, I'll go anywhere. Just make it clear."

As my course had gradually come to an end, I had seen
my contemporaries beginning to get jobs lined up. This would
be their "security" for the coming year, or however long.
Personally, I didn't want that kind of security. To me it was
a mixed blessing. My brand of logic told me that the more
security I had in life, the less I would need to trust God – and
surely true and lasting security can only be found in Him. It
seemed to me that being forced to be dependent upon God
was an exciting position to be in (albeit occasionally frustrating
when I had no clear sense of leading), and I was prepared to

accept such a lifestyle and whatever He had in store for me.

So it was that during my last week on the course I was still clueless as to what would happen next. My prayer became more frustrated than ever: "Lord, please! I'm twenty-five, single, available, have no ties and I'm willing to go anywhere and do anything. I beg you, reveal your purposes for my life!"

Later that day someone passed me a note with a name and telephone number scribbled on it. A man had been trying to track me down. I rang him and we arranged to meet the next day. Was the answer about to come?

We met in central London. After introducing himself, he told me, "Simon, as I've been praying, the Lord has laid your name on my heart. How would you feel about working in Burundi?"

My heart began beating faster. I asked him to tell me more, and he explained to me about the great needs among the youth in Burundi and how the church there was desperate for trained personnel. My mind was working overtime. I told him at the end of our meeting that I would "be spiritual and pray about it", saying that I would get back to him in due course.

I began praying that if this was what God wanted me to do, He would give me a sign to confirm His will. The following Monday found me sitting at a desk in front of a computer at my old job, which my former employers had kept open for me. As I stared at the screen I wrestled with the Burundi question.

"God," I prayed silently, "if you want me to go to Burundi, then please give me a sign. I know it's a hell-hole war zone, and it will mean leaving everything – family, friends, money, security – and making radical changes in my life. But, I trust you. Just give me a sign!"

It was a specific prayer request, seeking a specific answer. Just to be clear, the nation of Burundi had no connection whatsoever with my job, so yes, I was asking God to do something extraordinary. If He answered clearly, then I'd go. It would mean letting go of everything I cherished and moving to a country with a different language, climate and culture. But the bottom line for me was that this was a prayer of complete surrender. I knew that God had been challenging me to give Him command of my whole life, and to give Him permission to do with it whatever He saw fit.

But how could the Lord possibly answer? Wasn't the demand for a sign about some obscure country in the heart of Africa a little unreasonable? Well, not long after praying, I took a phone call and a voice on the other end of the line asked me a question out of the blue which took my breath away:

"Do you know anyone who wants to work in Burundi?"

It was all I needed. This was my call. I was off…

Disturbing news

I ended my marketing job and prepared to leave loved ones, financial security, and all that was familiar to me. It was time to take some radical risks. But just a few days before my departure date I received some disturbing news. The same man who had recruited me rang up and apologized – the church in Burundi, he said, didn't want an evangelist/preacher after all. What they actually needed was a secretary for the Bishop. He apologized profusely but explained that this would be my expected role.

What?! I hung up the phone in confusion and disbelief. "Lord, what's going on? Have I got it wrong? Is this a huge mistake?"

But it was too late. I'd bought my ticket, had my farewell party, and I was ready to go. I was risking a great deal and would likely end up looking a complete idiot if things didn't work out. But I truly believed God had called me to Burundi. To refuse to go now would be an act of disobedience as far as I was concerned.

The first stop on my journey was to fly into Rwanda, where I would spend four months acclimatizing in the company of my feisty aunt and granny, both of whom were working in the north of the country. Granny was an extremely hard-core missionary! She would be my language teacher, having spent half a century in Rwanda (the languages of Rwanda and Burundi were very similar). For the next four months I studied the language and pleaded with the Lord to release me from the job as the Bishop's administrator. What I really wanted to do was to work for Scripture Union (SU) in Burundi, because they worked predominantly with young people and were interdenominational. I wrote to all my friends back home to pray along those lines. Meanwhile, the team of workers at SU in Burundi received word that a *muzungu* (a white man) was coming to live in the area in a few months and wanted to join them, so they too began praying along similar lines.

The prayers and the study continued until, on my penultimate night in Rwanda, Granny prayed me off with the words: "Lord, Simon's surrendered to you. We've had enough of him! If you want to humble or teach him something in making him an administrative assistant, then so be it. We just ask that you'll overrule and make it clear."

I said goodbye to my Auntie Meg, Granny and the new friends I'd made, and headed for Rwanda's capital, Kigali, where I had arranged to drop into a particular guest house in the city to meet my boss who had flown in from the UK. I had only planned to be there a short time for a routine meeting, but after just ten minutes we were both amazed to bump into the head of SU in Burundi. He had just arrived to stay at the same guest house on his way to Tanzania, which was a further three days' drive away. Was this a coincidence? Surely not! What were the chances of three men from three different countries in transit to two other nations, who were praying for the same thing, and whose paths had crossed at such an opportune moment in the same small guest house in a bustling capital city? We praised God together, clearly seeing His hand at work, and committed the future to Him. Afterwards, I drove to a friend's house to spend my last night in Rwanda, thrilled with the anticipation of how God might intervene to free me up to work for SU.

That was my hope. At the moment the reality was that I was still lined up for a job in an alien country at war – and a job that I wasn't skilled for and didn't want to do anyway! Easy prey in an unknown and hostile environment, I'd had a lot of my money stolen and I was down to my last few hundred dollars in the world. I knew virtually no one, had given up everything, and had no idea how things would turn out. Yet, in the midst of such precariousness and uncertainty, I experienced a "nervous peace". I had peace, because I knew God had to be faithful, and it was a "nervous" peace because things were totally out of my hands. Nevertheless, I felt something significant was about to happen. I'd risked my all and surrendered everything to God. I knew He would be faithful and honor my trust in Him.

I managed to hitch a ride the next day down to Burundi with some friends. As we crossed the border and came down through the mountains, I caught sight of Bujumbura nestled below in the plain next to Lake Tanganyika, with a mesmerizing sunset melting over the Congolese peaks beyond. It was breathtaking. This was my new home for the foreseeable future. I was stricken by the sense that I was utterly vulnerable and at the mercy of forces beyond my control. But what a wonderful position of complete dependence and weakness to be in and be able to see the hand of God at work! My diary records:

20 January 1999: This is my new home – for one year? Two years? Ten? Fifty? Bizi Imana (God knows). Full of excitement, tired, nervous, exhilarated. It's so beautiful – but what a mess...

On my first day in Burundi I found an internet café and was able to send my first ever email from Burundi to friends and family, telling them how excited I was at God's leading. He was paving the way for me to work at SU, but SU was bankrupt and needed a computer. I sent that email off – the first of many thousands over the coming years – and received a prompt reply from a civil servant friend in London who was ecstatic as he wrote:

> I can't believe it! This sort of stuff never happens to me! This morning I prayed to God and told him that I wanted to give my computer to somebody and could he show me who it was. Then I logged on and got your email asking for a computer!

Sign after sign came to show that God was in charge. He was utterly faithful, supplying "all my needs according to his glorious riches in Christ Jesus" (Philippians 4:19). As C. S. Lewis says, "God gives where He finds empty hands." I was certainly empty-handed, vulnerable, weak and dependent on His mercy. But in such a position it was wonderful to observe Him intervene. And so began my incredible adventure in Burundi.

The context

For a more detailed recounting of Burundi's history there are a number of other sources you could turn to (such as René Lamarchand's *Burundi: Ethnic Conflict and Genocide*, CUP, 1994) but here I just want to give you a succinct summary of the context in which I found myself at the beginning of my time there.

Burundi used to be part of what was called Ruanda-Urundi until 1962 when Belgium, as the former colonial power, granted independence to both Rwanda and Burundi. These two lands are made up of three tribes: the majority Hutu (about 85 per cent of the population), the minority Tutsi (about 14 per cent), and the totally marginalized Twa (pygmies, about 1 per cent). Belgium had pursued a policy of privileging Tutsis, seeing them as more naturally adept at business, politics and administration, whilst considering Hutus more backward and naturally inclined towards agriculture. So up until 1962 these two nations had a shared history, but since that date things have been very different.

In Burundi, towards the end of the 1960s, the Tutsi minority tribe consolidated their power and sifted the army of Hutu elements, particularly in the upper echelons of leadership. By 1972, with Hutu being marginalized at every level of influence in society, including access to education, there was an uprising which was quashed by the Tutsi army. Throughout the country the army visited secondary schools and called out all Hutu students. These were taken away in trucks and never seen again. Although the numbers killed in the 1972 genocide are uncertain, the International Committee of Jurists' estimation was 100,000 in a population of approximately 4 million, half what it is today.

The impact of that genocide was to wipe out two generations of Hutu leadership in the country. Hundreds of thousands of Hutu fled to Congo and Tanzania and spent many years in squalid refugee camps, whilst any educated Hutu who remained in Burundi were in great danger of assassination. The Tutsi, as the minority, sought total domination in order to ensure their survival.

The rest of the 1970s and much of the 1980s were relatively peaceful, but this was largely because of strong Tutsi leadership, totally emasculated Hutu opposition, and a Tutsi-dominated military ready to intervene at the slightest sign of insurrection. This duly happened in the North in 1988 when Hutu resentment boiled over into rioting and murdering of

Tutsi, which was followed, just as in 1972, with the army more than simply restoring law and order. Helicopters and armored vehicles paved the way for troops to penetrate the hills and exact revenge. It is estimated that 15,000 Hutu were killed in the days that followed, many of whom were innocent. But unlike 1972, the response of the international community was immediate. Whereas US policy in Burundi had been to avoid involvement in any way in the political process back in 1972, this time the US House of Representatives issued a strongly worded resolution condemning the attacks and putting significant pressure on the government. Although the Burundian President, Buyoya, had initially denied the ethnic dimension, the accumulated international pressure compelled him to address the ethnic question, and changes in policy were gradually forced onto his agenda.

International pressure continued to be exerted on Burundi, so that by 1993 free multi-party national elections were organized. Naturally, in an ethnically polarized state, a leader from the majority tribe was bound to be chosen, and so it was that Melchior Ndadaye, a Hutu, won 65 per cent of the votes compared to Buyoya's 33 per cent. The handover of power for the first time to a Hutu president looked full of potential for the rebuilding of the nation. One Western embassy described the situation as "one of the most remarkable transitions to democracy yet seen in Africa", whilst another added that Burundi was "a model for all aspiring democracies".

Ruling minorities will always see democracy as both a threat and a recipe for legitimizing oppression by the majority. This is just what Tutsi felt in Burundi. The Hutu, on the other hand, having been subjugated to Tutsi hegemony for three decades, demanded proportional representation and corrective redressing of imbalances in the spheres of business, the judiciary and the army. This was the challenge to Ndadaye – to effect changes which satisfied the demands of the majority whilst appeasing the fears of the minority, and this in the fragile context of a nascent democracy underpinned by an opposition military.

In retrospect, it is difficult to see how the army could have been expected to remain orderly and to passively support what in practice was a direct loss and dissolution of their power and authority. Disastrously, a coup was carried out on 21 October 1993 by several senior Tutsi officers in the army. Ndadaye was killed and the country was plunged into turmoil. Hutu vented their spontaneous anger throughout the hills by indiscriminately murdering many thousands of Tutsi. The army's restoring of law and order was similar to 1972 and 1988 in its ruthlessness and arbitrariness, and upwards of 100,000 people died over the following two months.

What emerged from the carnage was the Tutsi reasserting total control over the nation. These events were to have a key bearing on political developments in neighboring Rwanda, and the genocide perpetrated there by Hutu on Tutsi in April 1994 was inextricably linked. Hutu in Rwanda could see the dangers posed by the Tutsi, and Hutu extremists incited the ultimate plan of complete annihilation of the Tutsi to end the ongoing ethnic problem.

With regards to Burundi, Hutu rebel groups began forming, from refugee camps in Tanzania and Congo as well as within Burundi itself. Buyoya returned to power in a coup in 1996, which was welcomed by most people because the President at the time had lost control of the army. The international community refused to recognize the legitimacy of Buyoya's administration, so an embargo was imposed, which lasted for two years. This resulted in the already destitute and practically bankrupt economy being further crippled.

In late January 1999, this was the situation I encountered upon my arrival. Burundi had been brought to its knees economically. The rebels were paralyzing any business activities by ambushing vehicles on the roads. I was handed an Amnesty International report cataloguing endless human rights violations. Dissent was not tolerated, so you had to watch what you said, and a number of rebel groups were doing their best to overthrow a vastly superior national army. The conflict had been going on for six long years, but there was absolutely no end in sight. Would we ever see peace come to Burundi? Would there be a return to full-scale war? What on earth was I doing there? Time would tell...

2

A RECKLESS FAITH?

Future plans are uncertain, but we all know that there is first
God's plan to be lived, and we can safely leave everything to
Him, "carefully careless" of it all.

Oswald Chambers

Jehovah Jireh
25 February 1999

I've been here just over a month now. The Bishop of
Bujumbura recognized God's engineering of circumstances
and graciously released me to work for SU. After my first few
nights at a Catholic guest house I met a lovely German couple
(Juergen and Monika) who run a guest house of their own. I
can stay with them for very little money and eat with them
and therefore not be too lonely. That's a relief. I initially told
my SU colleagues that I planned to live in the slum, but they
laughed and told me I'd be dead in minutes, that it was plain
stupidity.

I have borrowed a bicycle from another missionary and
this will be my mode of transport to get around the town. I

will be the only white man in the country to cycle to work, but at this stage it is all I can afford. I know it will be hard, sweaty work in this oppressive humidity.

On my first weekend, eight of us piled onto SU's rickety team van and drove into the hills for two days of outreach. We traveled along reputedly the most dangerous road in Burundi at the moment and broke down four times during the journey! These were tense moments, to say the least, with very few other vehicles traveling this main business artery to the rest of the country. The constant delays meant we missed a whole day of outreach. I was furious that people missed out on hearing the gospel just because we didn't have a half-decent vehicle.

When we eventually returned to our base I wrote to all my contacts and asked them to help us get out of debt and buy a functional vehicle. I pictured $25,000 as the need and decided to give it a month. That month has now elapsed and the money has miraculously come in, with one gift of $8,000 alone made out specifically for a new vehicle! I love this adventure of faith!

Planning in faith
7 April 1999

Due to the fact that SU has been basically bankrupt for the last decade, they haven't run a youth Bible camp in years. However, in faith we decided to plan one. The build-up was exciting. We sent out invitations to dozens of schools, yet we had nothing in our bank account, so we needed God to provide. Ten days before the event was due to take place, we had our monthly all-day prayer meeting. At about 3 p.m., as we were praying about funding for the camp, I sensed God saying that we'd get the money and that as a sign, when I got home there would be a message waiting for me, promising funds. It would have been easy to take that on board but keep such a word to myself, but I took a chance and shared with the group that I believed God had just reassured me, and that on Monday I would come to the office with the money. Back home, I eagerly and nervously accessed my email. Sure enough, there was a message promising the money we needed. God is so faithful.

This whole episode taught me two things: firstly, that we need to persevere in prayer. How often do we really wrestle in prayer to see God intervene? I think often He desires to know just how desperately we want something and whether we're willing to trust Him to provide it. Secondly, I learnt again that all the answers to our prayers come by God's grace alone. I don't want to give the impression that I am some giant of the faith. In truth, for most of the day my prayers were feeble, half-hearted and unbelieving. I remember thinking how utterly pathetic and limp I was being. Yet, God in His grace answered nonetheless.

The day of the camp arrived. Many of those in attendance were leaders of student Christian Unions, so they were a seriously passionate crowd and the times of sung worship were amazing. The living conditions in the camp were basic in the extreme. It was very cold at night and the mosquitoes had a field day, meaning that a number of people fell ill with both dysentery and malaria. I was reasonably well protected from the elements, sleeping in my tent. But the food was dire and hygiene standards in the "kitchen" were outrageous, so I was happy to escape with a two-day bout of diarrhea.

On the second morning, the Holy Spirit convicted a number of people of the need to repent. It started with a teacher and then all sorts of people came forward. One girl confessed she had slept with a priest to get the money for her school fees (all of $5, but it represents a large sum of money out here). Like this girl, many have to sleep with their teachers to pass their exams or pay their fees. It's a desperate state of affairs, but I understand their dilemma. If they don't cooperate then they simply have no future; they won't be able to attain any level of qualification or get a job.

What victory there is in such public confession! There was much rejoicing. The schedule went out of the window as the Lord set the agenda. Late the next afternoon, during a seminar on AIDS, a girl was taken outside to be prayed for. You could hear her screams for the next several hours as a whole load of demons were cast out of her. She returned later to testify to God's glory, a transformed woman!

After five days together everyone returned to their respective schools with renewed vision and passion for the work, knowing God had been in our midst. My boss commented that in the last fifteen years of youth work he had never seen the Lord move in such power.

The cheapness of life
5 June 1999

I've recently bought a 250cc Honda off-road motorbike to get around the schools more easily. (This week someone pointed out to me that the number plate was "007". I hadn't noticed it, but will try to live up to my name!) I love it, but the roads out here are extremely dangerous and seem to be governed by the law of the jungle – i.e. the bigger vehicle always has priority! You can forget about what the actual law says. It's fair enough, I guess. So I'm always the smaller one, apart from bicycles.

Yesterday, late morning, as I drove along I encountered a dead or unconscious bloodstained body on the road. While everyone else was driving past, I stopped and dragged him off the road. I flagged down a man with a truck and told him I would pay him to take the man to hospital. I followed on my bike. When we reached the hospital, I rushed in, unsure as to whether the victim was still alive or not. I shouted for help but the nurses nonchalantly carried on eating their food and said we'd have to wait – it was still lunch break. Can you believe it? Life is so cheap here. But then again, they only get paid $20 per month – not enough to really care. I popped by today and the man looks like he's going to be fine, thankfully.

In the afternoon after that incident, my co-worker Freddy and I went to the market and bought matching pairs of sunglasses for fun (since we spend a lot of time on the motorbike traveling around the country). He's my new best friend here and is becoming a real soulmate. I believe God has given us each other as we share the same reckless passion to see young lives transformed.

Freddy is the only boy from his village in the bush to have graduated from primary school. He used to walk two hours each way to and from school. He never wore shoes or underpants until the age of fourteen. What pushed Freddy into working for SU was an incident a few years ago at the school upcountry where he was teaching. Someone threw a grenade into a dormitory and six young lads were blown up. Freddy helped carry out some of the dead and vowed he had to mobilize the youth countrywide to follow a different way. He sold his two cows and came to Bujumbura. He's been working for the last three years before my arrival without any salary, just trusting the Lord.

He said to me, "Simon, we live by faith, not by sight. Sometimes I've gone days without eating. I've learnt to fast voluntarily and involuntarily. For the last three years I've had just one of everything – one pair of shoes, one pair of underpants, one pair of trousers and one shirt. That's it. People said I was crazy, but I know God is faithful."

God is faithful indeed. Now I've been able to get Freddy a salary and we're seeing amazing fruit all over the country as we travel far and wide. Our budget is so tight, however, that we often sleep together in some very grim places. Recently we had to share a single bed and I woke up with my face in his armpit!

Risking our lives
21 June 1999

Lots of people are dying in ambushes on the roads right now. You can travel up what should be the busiest trade route in the country and go half an hour without seeing a single person or vehicle apart from the soldiers in their dug-outs. One night recently Freddie and I were in the middle of nowhere at midnight, driving through the bush. It seemed lunacy, but we'd just shared our faith at a school and had received a huge response. It wasn't an option to stay overnight there, so we had little choice but to drive back to the nearest town. It was a strange and eerie feeling, yet we were so full of joy. People can't believe we take such risks, but we simply must, and to me those risks are absolutely vindicated by the results.

Yesterday we returned on the motorbike from the South and all had seemed calm. However, a UN report in the evening showed that about forty people had been killed on that very road in several ambushes, while we had come through unscathed with no sign of trouble. The rebels must have seen us, but let us through for whatever reason. Maybe the Lord blinded them to our passing?

Today I was particularly troubled as to whether to pull out of a planned trip to a school upcountry. It's interesting, because Freddy is absolutely convinced before God that we'll be protected wherever we go. He has no qualms whatsoever. I'm not at all afraid to die, but I don't sense any guarantee from God that He'll stop us from being killed – after all, plenty of wonderful people of faith have died in the call of duty throughout history, so why should we be exempt? I had lunch with Juergen and Monika and they strongly urged me to cancel the trip. I didn't feel I could. I packed my bags, got on the bike, and was just about to leave when Juergen ran out of the house and pleaded with me one last time. I found the look in his eyes oddly comforting. It was nice to know someone really cared. No one outside the country understands quite how dangerous it is here right now and how risky these trips are, so it felt good to see him desperately concerned for my safety. I agreed, got off the bike and rang Freddy to cancel the trip. He simply chuckled to himself about it and said "OK", whilst his faithful wife Josée was mightily relieved!

Hard-core common sense
17 October 1999

We're up in Matana doing a weekend of outreach. There are lots and lots of very long meetings taking place. Someone known to my co-workers died recently, so they went to visit relatives and share condolences. I stayed and played with the four kids in the home I'm lodging in. We had a great time and laughed a lot. This is what life would be like if I lived permanently upcountry – no privacy at all. Each of them was looking through all my things and throwing a ball around the room, making a complete nuisance of themselves. They loved it and I sort of did too.

I also had an hour to pray by myself in the dark and experienced real intimacy with the Spirit, crying out in desperation. I've been reading a book about C. T. Studd that I've found profoundly stirring. Quite apart from working in China and India for umpteen years, having given up *all* of a *massive* personal inheritance, and fleeing the adulation of the whole nation as the best English cricketer of his day – it's the pioneer evangelism in the heart of Africa that blows me away! He ignored the advice of every single person around him, including his wife, because he knew the Lord was calling him. Suffering from chronic asthma, and in his fifties, he still trekked 700 miles through the Zairian jungle for two years, surveying the needs. He spent eighteen years there, seeing numerous tribes reached with the gospel. He moved forward without any financial security, because nobody would back him, and trusted the Lord to provide for every need, praying and waiting on God from 3:30 each morning. He even worked tirelessly to have the New Testament translated into the local dialect whilst on his deathbed, working up to eighteen hours a day. He experienced so many setbacks, hardships, trials and rejections, but saw an indigenous mission movement established.

What a challenge! I can hardly relate to the man – he is far too hard-core for me! And yet I want to relate to him. I want to do absolutely everything for the Lord, because He is worth everything. Of course, I want to hold on to common sense. But the Lord does not work on the basis of common sense! That is so clear to me. The good is the enemy of the best. Common sense will so often rationalize and steer us towards averageness and lukewarmness. I shouldn't think there ever was a man or woman of God who achieved anything of note for the Lord who followed the path of common sense at key decision-making times. I'm bored of people telling me to be careful. Indeed, I'm bored of being careful. I want to be recklessly effective in Christ's service and work by kingdom dynamics. Better go out with guns blazing! What a God we serve: awesome, precious, holy, risen Jesus! Holy Spirit, I beg you to fill me. I so need your touch, anointing, empowering and leading!

Oswald Chambers in *My Utmost for His Highest* says this:

The simplicity that comes from our natural common sense decisions is apt to be mistaken for the witness of the Spirit, but the Spirit witnesses only to His own nature and to the work of redemption, never to our own reason. If we try to make Him witness to our reason, it is no wonder that we are in darkness and perplexity. Fling it all overboard, trust in God, and He will give the witness.

Living hell
22 October 1999

The situation here is just horrific and the scale of suffering overwhelming. I hear gunfire nearly every day and on one occasion it felt much too close for comfort. The UN have evacuated all non-emergency staff following the ambushing of their convoy last week (thirteen dead, including two expats). These ambushes occur nearly daily; people are dropping like flies in their thousands.

Far worse is the number of displaced people. The latest Government policy has been to force several hundred thousand people around the capital into internally displaced camps. They have literally rounded up everyone like cattle and forced them into given areas. The idea is that anyone outside of the camps is considered a rebel and killed. But this policy has been disastrous. People who were already extremely poor have been uprooted from their homes, which have been pillaged in their absence. They depend on the land, but have been taken away from it and prevented from continuing to work. So now they're starving to death. They're supposedly under the "protection" of Government troops, but the latter are from the other tribe and are therefore exacerbating the problem by raping the women and instilling a climate of total fear. So many are dying here and the international community is being kept in the dark, or is choosing not to get involved.

Just try to imagine this: according to the statistics I've been shown, about 260,000 people have been herded into several dozen different enforced, internally displaced camps within a few miles of here. Many of these people own nothing in the world but the stinking clothes on their backs. In the camps there is no water (literally, in some cases, for the first week), no food, no toilets (just try to picture that when it is forbidden to leave the camp in a month), no shelter from the lashing rains and relentless sun. Disease is rife. I wonder if there is a single place on earth where there is more concentrated suffering right now? I'm not exaggerating.

Juergen and Monika's nanny, Odetta, had a narrow escape during the turmoil. As soldiers were busy rounding up her family she was able to call Monika for help. Monika drove up the hillside (at considerable personal risk) to plead on Odetta's behalf. As a white person, Monika was an embarrassment to the soldiers, who told her to go away. Monika asked that Odetta and her baby be allowed to come back to our house. The soldier she was speaking to refused and forced Monika to leave. But when she had arrived back at our place, within minutes there was a frantic knocking at the door. It was Odetta. She had decided to risk her life and run for it as soon as the soldier's back was turned. She had run down the hill in terror with her baby on her back in a matter of minutes, at what must have been near world-record speed. Now we have her and about five others sleeping in a shelter in our back garden. The conditions are pretty grim, but they are miles better than in the death camps up in the hills.

It's hard to see many positives here: there's a heavy blanket of despair and hopelessness hanging over the nation. I find myself being affected by it as well. Over the last few weeks I've had a bout of dysentery, back problems, some flu and have been bitten by a dog.

Recently I exposed a local corruption scandal and the aftermath has been highly draining and emotionally exhausting. We live in a culture ruled by fear. Although everyone knew it was taking place, nobody wanted to put their lives at risk. I just couldn't go on seeing God's money misappropriated, so I spoke to the organization's head office in the USA and their local point person was whisked out of the country – but not before the corrupt individual in question (supposedly a "man of God", a pastor!) tried to kill her. It means I'm having to watch my back at the moment, particularly when driving around on the motorbike. The easiest way to get rid of me would be to arrange an "accident" on the road.

Ready to die
24 December 1999

My morning meditation was on Colossians 3:3, which talks of one's life being hidden in Christ. Oswald Chambers puts it so well, something I rejoice in being able to relate and testify to:

> When you really see Jesus, I defy you to doubt Him. When He says, "Let not your hearts be troubled," if you see Him I defy you to trouble your mind. It is a moral impossibility to doubt when He is there. Every time you get into personal contact with Jesus, His words are real. "My peace I give you," it is a peace all over from the crown of the head to the sole of the feet, an irrepressible confidence. "Your life is hid with Christ in God," and the imperturbable peace of Jesus Christ is imparted to you.

It's a wonderful position to be in. I'm ready to die and think about dying every day (without being morbid) because I'm surrounded by death, but there's nothing like having this peace. I feel utterly privileged. Thank you, Lord.

3

ROOM FOR HOPE

When you say a situation or a person is hopeless, you are
slamming the door in the face of God.

Charles L. Allen

Fruit in the gloom
2 January 2000

Christmas and New Year's Eve have come and gone and it
was all unbelievably hectic. We hosted an amazing street kids'
party, launched an AIDS project, conducted seminars and
promoted and distributed the coming year's Bible reading
notes nationwide. On top of all that there was lots of traveling,
preaching and showing of evangelistic films, and we ran a
four-day Bible camp for around 150 schoolkids. So much
activity in such a short space of time means I am noticeably
washed out and grumpy. I'm in desperate need of a break – as
much for those around me as for myself!

The economy here is barely functional, corruption is
increasing, and there is the daily tension of knowing the
simmering undercurrent of unrest might erupt into full-

scale war at any moment. Recently, while playing rugby on the beach with some lads and swimming thirty yards from a hippo, I looked up into the hills at one of the camps where refugees and displaced people are dying every day. It was an utterly surreal moment, and yet it is so very, very real.

It's certainly not all doom and gloom here. How could it be when so many are coming to know the Lord Jesus? It's almost exactly one year since I joined SU under such God-ordained circumstances and it's awesome to look back and see what He has done. Yet again, on this latest camp, His Spirit came upon us such that we were on our knees, weeping in His presence at our own sinfulness and the desperate state of the nation.

As grim as it gets
16 January 2000

It's 1.58 p.m. and I have just returned from an amazing morning. In a couple of hours I am off to preach again and show a film at a youth outreach, but I wanted to get this down on paper while my memory is still fresh and my emotions are still high. I picked up Celestin on the motorbike and drove southwards out of Bujumbura to a displacement camp. He's an interesting man – clearly totally traumatized from his recent experiences, yet he's chosen to come back to Burundi from Kenya where he's been studying for several years. He obtained a valuable degree in the process and wants to use it to benefit his people in this land, even though it would have been much safer to keep his family in Kenya. In the meantime his house has been razed to the ground and his wider family have been either killed or forced to flee the country.

We had the usual adrenaline rush caused by traveling on dangerous roads, always with the potential for numerous hazards. We arrived at the camp, but weren't allowed in without a letter from the authorities. Celestin, however, knew the military chief because he'd been here a few months ago to sort things out when his brother was killed, so we managed, relatively painlessly, to get a letter allowing us entry. This was no small thing, bearing in mind that outsiders are not meant to see what is going on here. There were tens of thousands in this camp, which had started near the road, but had subsequently been shifted behind the next hill to keep it out of the sight of anyone who might want to alert the outside world. All of the people in the camp had to leave their homes several months ago. Now they're allowed out just once a week to go to their fields.

The purpose of our trip was to minister at a church that had been established in the camp itself. People swarmed around us as we pulled up next to its makeshift building, loosely constructed from sticks tied together and with some UN plastic sheeting spread over the top. We spoke to the pastor and he told us that about ten people die here every day, mainly from cholera. I'm amazed these people manage to smile at all. Materially speaking, they have nothing left in the world. Disease is rife here, so after we preached about a third of the people who came forward wanted prayer for healing. We saw many heads and faces with ringworm, heard the constant bleating of babies, and smelled the pungent aromas of so many unwashed bodies huddled together. I touched and held hands with beautiful little filthy, skinny children, who grinned demurely, avoiding any eye contact.

I preached on where our hope comes from: "The Lord, the Maker of heaven and earth" (Psalm 121:1–2). Standing on the crest of the hill, I had an awesome view as I preached. Beyond the faces staring avidly at me was the glorious panorama of Lake Tanganyika, several hundred feet below, stretching across to the majestic and serene Congolese mountains in the distance. What a visual testimony to this wonderful Maker, whilst under our noses was an altogether different testimony to the mess mankind has made.

A large number of these dear folk responded to the message. We then had a quick lunch in a shack, perhaps six feet by four feet, which was where a family of eight slept. I didn't want to eat their food, as I knew how scarce it was, and realized that others wouldn't eat if I did. But to refuse would have been an insult, so I had the acceptable minimum. It was the most costly meal of my life. Sitting under the scorching sun with a tin roof overhead felt like being in an oven – we were all pouring with sweat. Looking up, I could see that the tin strips had been pierced systematically every few inches. This was done on purpose by looting Government soldiers who were meant to be protecting the people. Because they were from the "other" tribe, they wanted to make sure that the roof would leak when it rained; hopefully then the people would die quicker. Why, oh why? Nearing the end of our visit, I was further humbled when our hosts forced us to take a bunch of bananas back with us. They gave us so much out of the little they had. What a challenge to those of us who have so much.

When we were done I didn't want to hang around. Down the hill forty civilians were killed on New Year's Eve on their way to the market. Up the hill two weeks ago there had been fierce battling and the rebels had sent back down the severed heads of the soldiers they'd killed. Celestin pointed to a place very near to us and said that even the soldiers were scared to go there. Conceivably, half a mile away from us were guerrilla forces preparing for their next onslaught. We didn't want to risk being exposed to any of it. We could see that there was blood freshly spilled on the road since we'd been there in the last few hours, and other dark patches along the way told of similar but less recent tales of woe. As we sped past the landmark monument where Stanley supposedly met Livingstone back in 1867, we came across a group of soldiers on patrol who had obviously been on the job – they had crazed looks in their eyes – so we kept going.

All this subliminal tension is extremely tiring. I really am exhausted. But how dare I moan when I have so much? I want to cry my eyes out for those cute little faces which mask such untold suffering, grief and degradation, but I fear my tears are a mechanism to absolve myself of my relentlessly nagging feelings of guilt; guilt that I have a roof over my head that doesn't leak, a meal more than once every couple of days, a change of clothes (or ten), a healthy body, the freedom to get to safety if I want to, enough money to be able to afford to make choices, etc. As if a few tears will show that I care and am with them in their struggles. And yet I suppose it's what we do with what we have that really counts…

What needs changing in my life, Lord? Once I've worked out the answer to that question, give me the courage to obey what You say.

Briefly, I'm tempted to jack it all in, to go back to sanitized and safe England, to family and friends, to an equally needy and infinitely more spiritually bankrupt society in the West which has everything to live with and nothing to live for. But no, it's better to be here where God has placed me.

"I'll cut out your eyes!"
17 January 2000

There has been a strike called for by various syndicates, so everyone is on high alert and expecting an imminent outbreak of violence. At the office I encountered, yet again, a strange man called Aloise who has been bothering me lately, asking for money. He came to my house once before and I gave him some Bible-reading notes. Apparently, that wasn't good enough, as he'd come back again. There was something unnerving about him. I'd told him that I'd rather we met at the office than at my home, since I didn't really know who he was. When he approached me today I was in a bad mood because

I was facing some difficulties with my visa and didn't want to get sucked into a long discussion, so I simply excused myself and drove back to the immigration office, where I pleaded for a hearing with the big chief.

As I left home for the office in the afternoon a man flagged me down on the road and gave me a letter which he insisted I read on the spot and reply to. It was from Aloise, basically making death threats. Either I should give him money, he said, or face the consequences. He said he knew my game, that SU were deceiving the Burundian people. Plus, as I'd been rude to him in the morning, he told me that if I didn't reconsider it would cost me "the eyes of my head". His messenger wanted a reply there and then, but I told him I was in a hurry and he could come and talk to me at the office. When I arrived, I shared the letter with my colleagues, who didn't treat it too seriously.

Arriving back home, I found another letter waiting for me. This one was a bit confusing. It was from a man down the street who said he'd overheard two others talking about me, saying they were demanding 100,000 Burundian francs ($100), or else they'd kill me. He said I shouldn't pay even one franc, as they were just crooks. But one of them had tried to force entry into the house, which had naturally scared Odetta. Only the barking dogs had deterred the intruder.

I also heard that Aloise was apparently due to turn up at the house around 6 p.m., and after a sit-down meeting with Juergen and Monika, we decided it would be better if I wasn't around. I rang my friend Mike, the US Security Chief, and he agreed that I could stay with him for the night.

Comedy grenade chase
18 January 2000

I hardly slept at all. I was too restless, with many thoughts whirling around my head. The Bishop's wife got wind of what was happening and connected me with the Chief of Police. He was out when I phoned, but his assistant gave an audible gulp as I explained the reason why I was phoning. There were two other expats currently receiving death threats, but both of them were guilty of sleeping with the aggrieved person's wife, which I hadn't done, and the sums demanded for them were $2,000 and $3,000 respectively. I was rather offended that the demands made to me were only to the tune of $100!

The Chief rang me back and I abandoned my language studies to go and see him. I showed him the letters. He said that if the unsavory characters arrived at the office or the house, I should stall them whilst the police were contacted, and they would come and arrest them. We had a good discussion. He seemed a nice man and was a good contact for me to have for the future. But, I returned home only to find Aloise waiting outside my door with a grenade in his hand. From a distance Leopold, the house guard, signaled that I shouldn't approach. What followed then was almost surreal comedy. I ran across the road to Brad and Vicky's house (US missionaries), phoned the police and told them what was happening so they would come and arrest the man. They rang back a few moments later to say we would have to go and pick them up, as they didn't have a car! I then rang Monika, asking her to come and pick me up. She came out of the house next door (they are No. 10 and I am No. 8), right past Aloise with his grenade. She arrived in their pathetic little jeep, with two kids' seats squeezed into the back. We drove quickly into town and, after getting lost a few times, eventually found the police station, picked up two soldiers (me and one of them huddled very uncoolly in the kids' seats in the back), and off we went, scouring the streets. Of course, all this had taken so long that Aloise had long since disappeared! My description of him didn't give the police much to go on, either. All I could say was that he was a black man wearing a cap. Everyone is black here, half are men, and in the rain maybe a third were wearing caps. The Police had their work cut out!

Back in the thick of it
26 January 2000

I've just had a wonderful week's break in Uganda with Ed Walker, who works with Tearfund. I needed to get out of the stressful environment that is my norm and hoped this would also help to get my nasty acquaintance off my trail. We hired a car and went to Kabale and Kisiizi. I awoke one night screaming, mid-nightmare – because of the threats – and Ed gave me short shrift, grunting at me to be quiet before rolling over for more sleep. We had a good chuckle about it in the morning, with Ed telling me (in jest) to stop being such a softy. I'll know where not to go for sympathy in future!

Today we have returned to Burundi and are back in the thick of things. I'm glad to hear that Aloise hasn't shown his face for a while. Thank you, Lord, for a truly wonderful break, although we didn't rest much at all – it was all action, which is how I love it. But this is my home now. Monika was surprised that I was happy to be back. The love I feel for this place must be from the Lord. There is so little otherwise to endear it to one. Many of the people I interact with are devious, manipulative, dishonest, ruthless, back-stabbing, corrupt and malicious. But despite all that, I do love this land. African men and women outside Burundi whom we have talked to over the last few days have oohed and ahhed when they've heard we work here. Isn't it a bit dangerous? Is there any light at the end of the tunnel? Will there ever be peace? I long to be a part of it all the way. Yet now I'm back – and I'm honestly glad to be back – I suddenly feel so oppressed and heavy again. I could quite easily burst into tears right now, all the more after reading mail from my loved ones. Can I last many more years here – in terms of burn-out, let alone not being killed?

Room for hope?
5 April 2000

Tensions have been rising between the Government and the rebels. It needs to be remembered that this Government is illegitimate. It came into being following a *coup d'état* and the rebels are waging a legitimate war in pursuit of the re-establishment of democratic rule. Often in the West we think in terms of a government representing the good guys and rebels being the bad guys, but that simply isn't the case here. Both sides are engaged in a messy, bloody conflict with multiple abuses, which neither can win, and in the meantime many innocent civilians are caught in the crossfire. The thing is, the Tutsi army is trying to flush out Hutu rebels and they accuse the Hutu civilians of hiding and protecting the rebels. The civilians are caught between a rock and a hard place. They get killed by the rebels if they don't give them food and money. So they have no choice, but then often end up getting killed by the army as rebel sympathizers. It's tragic. Things have got progressively worse on a national level. Recently I sent out the following appeal for prayer:

Please pray for this nation!

I hope all is well your end. Things here, on a personal level, are fine – no more death threats. SU is seeing awesome fruit in the schools, we have a united team, and I won the Burundi Squash Championship last weekend(!) – but the situation in the nation is deteriorating further, if that is possible. Inflammatory demonstrations are planned for tomorrow, the petrol shortage is crippling the already defunct economy, several hundred thousand people are still languishing in enforced camps within a few miles of here and rebels have just sent down the heads of seven Government soldiers with their respective ID cards stapled to their ears. The peace talks in Arusha are supposedly coming to a climax, although whatever the outcome is, some groups have already rejected it. Nelson Mandela, as negotiator, has his work cut out and the consensus is that if the talks fail, it will be disastrous. Burundi is already a nation at war, but instead of the current steady trickle who are dying, it will mean tens of thousands dying almost overnight – bloody carnage – and everything will be back to square one. Let's stand against it in Jesus' name.

A diary entry will spare you my ramblings:

8 February: Yesterday's demonstrations were quashed mercilessly at the start, as the guys involved were seemingly wanting to start an out-and-out riot to trash the city and undermine the peace talks. They were all arrested and given a severe shoeing in prison – their form of punishment generally receiving a positive verdict from most people!

I'm reading a book on heroes of the faith. What is the sacrifice? Back in 1857, David Livingstone (who dropped everything to go to Africa and suffered hugely in seeking to open Africa up for commerce rather than slavery) concluded: "I never made a sacrifice." I agree. Our pursuit in coming out here in obedience to God is not entirely selfless; we will receive a hundredfold (Mark 10:28–30), and anyway, being in His will brings incomparable peace, fulfillment, joy and security.

Security? Yes, even in one of the most dangerous places on earth. Without wishing to sound morbid, I've done lots more thinking about death. How selfish I am, wanting to be with Jesus, whilst family and friends would mourn (perhaps that's wishful thinking!) and not understand. How much more work has the Lord for me to do here? "For me, to live is Christ and to die is gain" (Philippians 1:21). As followers of Christ, we are in a win/win situation. How real and relevant that whole passage is! Any trials must pale into insignificance in comparison with His surpassing glory that will be revealed in us. It just makes this gift of life so very urgent now.

And yes, it is a gift, not a right. Like my education, my financial means, my career choices, my freedom to share the gospel, my functional body – all of them are gifts, not rights; as is my ability to look out from here and see God's beautiful creation. The first threatening letter I received said that if I didn't comply with their requests for money, it would cost me my eyes, so I have been imagining being blind… it's a horrific thought. So thank you, Lord, for the gift of eyesight, and all the other gifts you shower on me, and may I not take them for granted. For us Brits, it's important to take on board, because our national pastime is moaning. We are outrageously blessed, yet still manage to find things that are wrong and complain about our glass being half empty. Or to use another metaphor, it's like in the West we have a clear blue sky with a small cloud in the distance and we complain about the cloud, whilst out here our African brothers have a cloudy sky with a small patch of blue, and they are grateful for that tiny break in the clouds.

So I resolve to be a grateful person, and I realize that actually, grateful people are usually happy people. Help me, Lord, to maximize these gifts whilst still in this "tent", whether it is home for another sixty years, or just another six months, or even six days. I do believe the Lord has assured me of protection through to the summer at least, although I may be wrong. When it comes to hearing such "words" and discerning whether they are from Him, I openly admit I'm a beginner.

The man speaking at Grandpa's funeral said of his urgency in gospel work: "Peter Guillebaud worked as if he'd live forever and he lived as if he'd die tomorrow." That challenges me because it's a constant struggle for an inherently lazy person like me to not waste my time. Still, it's easier to remember the urgency here in these grim surroundings than in the West, where suffering and death are perceived as affronts to our misconceived rights to immortality and blessing.

The Tearfund guests showed up – three of them – and I joined them for supper along with the Head of the European Union. It was interesting to listen to his views from an altogether different perspective, but depressing to reflect on the future of this nation. People say that Britain was spared something similar to the French Revolution because of the radical social reforms undertaken, primarily by Christians, in a period of revival a couple of centuries back. Well, there are blatantly troubles ahead for this nation unless the Lord intervenes in His miraculous power. When you consider that the population is set to double (to 12 million) by the year 2020, that agriculture is 35 years behind the rest of the world, that there are no pressure groups, so the Government can behave as it likes, that potential for economic growth is minimal in such unstable climes, that emotional wounds will take generations to heal, and that the church reflects the rancor, corruption and schisms of society at large, *where is the hope?* The answer is exactly where I preach from most often these days, Psalm 121: "the Lord, the Maker of heaven and earth".

God, please heal this nation! Bring lasting peace, true forgiveness, purity, integrity, unity in your bride – I beg you!

4

LIFE TO THE FULL

Many of the great achievements of the world were accomplished
by tired and discouraged men who kept on working.

John Sachs

Content with what?
5 September 2000

Living in a place like Burundi, one is constantly bombarded
with needs, and crises occur frequently. I find myself sending
out regular, urgent prayer requests like the following:

Men who want no mists must be content with the plains. But
give me the mountain! It will be but a little while, and, the mists
evaporated, the mountain will stand out in all its grandeur.

(attributed to Richard H. Froude)

Hi guys! I hope this finds you experiencing "life to the full"
– whatever Jesus meant by that – with its highs and lows, joy
and sadness, peaks and troughs. For what it's worth, I think
that He meant at least two things: (a) life was never meant to

be dull, because we have the bigger picture, and (b) it's not meant to be easy, but the end result is worth everything. So we aren't, we surely can't, we simply mustn't, be content with the plains.

A lot has happened in the last few months. I wanted to write now because, as always with this precious country, these are key times. Apparently we even made the news in the West, at least for a minute or two! On 28 August, fourteen out of the nineteen factions at the Arusha peace talks signed a provisional accord, with Mandela, Clinton and others in attendance. But people have low expectations of peace holding out. There have been high-profile political and military assassinations, riots, ambushes, arson, and grenade attacks.

My family was here for a visit two weeks ago. One morning, a grenade exploded a couple of hundred yards away. It was far more effective than my alarm clock for getting me out of bed! We wanted to go upcountry, but it simply wasn't safe enough. Yet, as I write, I'm experiencing a strange peace. It just doesn't make sense. At times, everything is so very normal. But the events of 1993 in Burundi (150,000+ killed), and 1994 in Rwanda (800,000+ killed), are being compared to what's going on right now. It could so easily be the same all over again. So please pray!

Today has already been eventful and produced a whole range of emotions. I was praying on the veranda when Abraham, who works here at the guest house, arrived. Yesterday, the rebels came yet again and took everything. They also burnt his clothes and other possessions or threw them in the river. The only things he has left in the world are the clothes on his back. The injustice and senselessness of it all make me mad. But, far worse than that, his five-year-old boy fled during all the shooting. His chances of survival were extremely slim and, for all we knew, he was already dead. We held out very little hope. So when Abraham arrived my heart was thumping with anticipation.

"Did you find him?" I blurted out.

Abraham revealed a huge grin. "Yes!" he exclaimed. "Praise the Lord!"

Evariste, my colleague at SU, had a very close shave a few days ago. He was caught in crossfire and had to dive into a drainage ditch and crawl for a kilometer in the filth, getting cut up in the process, while bullets pinged overhead between both sides. He lost his identity papers on the way and got accused of being a rebel as he reached the end of the danger zone. But later someone went back and found them all. Praise the Lord that he is still alive and well. He and Abraham are two of the people I see every day and care for deeply.

Our AIDS project is having a progressively bigger impact. When my co-worker Nathan did some seminars in Gitega, word spread about what was taking place and a couple of hundred people came, mostly uninvited. Among them were many prostitutes, of whom twenty-eight chose to renounce their profession and make a fresh start. Of these, fifteen made commitments to Christ! Cossette's children's ministry is taking off, as she gets around churches training up Sunday school teachers. There's the usual race against time to get the coming year's Bible-reading notes written, typed up and printed, ready for distribution before the end of the year. Plus we are opening up our first regional office to co-ordinate activities outside the capital more effectively. Basically, we are pushed to our limits.

Satan has not sat idly by all this time. An SU volunteer was shot dead in an ambush. Peter's little boy, Simon, died recently. The team had a serious car crash (mercifully, nobody was badly injured). On top of that there have been tensions in the office: personality clashes, rumors, lies and miscommunication have led on occasion to distrust and misunderstanding. Freddy and Joram have left and need to be replaced urgently. John, my boss, has a huge load on his shoulders and needs a lot of wisdom. Our relationship is absolutely key, because he is in charge, whilst I am the source of finance. I have been slandered as pro-Hutu, which is the easiest way for anyone to try to undermine my work. I miss Freddy and several other key people close to me, so things are a bit tougher. For the first time I am lonely out here quite often. But that's not a bad thing at all, because it means I am more reliant on God and spend more time with Him. It's pathetic how fickle my allegiance to Christ is.

But I mustn't give you a wrong picture of how tough it is here. What I find difficult to get my head around most of all is how poverty and opulence can sit side by side. I have several friends with swimming pools, so at any time I can take it easy and cool off. But a mile up the hill, people like Abraham live in fear of not waking up in the morning. I hate that. I hate, too, the way I drive past beggars and into the tennis club. Would Jesus have played tennis? Where would He have lived? I struggle with these issues every day. And, in this strange world I inhabit, as soon as I got back from England, I was selected to play for the Burundian national tennis team against Rwanda! It doesn't make sense! Can anybody help me out with the answers?

On a lighter note, I had a funny incident after one game of tennis last week: something jammed in the engine and my motorbike conked out. About forty times I tried kick-starting it again without success. I fiddled with the clutch and the petrol tank, but still had no joy. I was sweating like a pig by this stage. Three young men were talking to and laughing at me. It was dusk and I was getting concerned about being stranded outside so late. Almost in despair I slapped the bike and shouted, "In Jesus' name, I command you to start!" Immediately it roared into life and the lads gasped. I tried to look like I wasn't surprised and then we all laughed our heads off! "That's my Jesus!" I told them. "Do you know Him? He's powerful!"

Life to the full – it is not easy, but it's never dull and is worth everything! Content with the plains? No way! "But give me the mountain! It will be but a little while…"

Fog
22 September 2000

During the last couple of months I've felt like I am drowning in a fog of depression. It's something I have never experienced before. Things are not bad really, and I have so many reasons to be thankful for all God's blessings, but instead I can only see the bad side of every situation… every person… every potential scenario. I am broken and have no hope for anything. I know that this is the onslaught of the evil one, but I feel pathetically apathetic and hollow.

I suppose a lot of it stems from sticky relationships at work. We're growing very fast at SU and seeing phenomenal things happen, but one of the key players is very dysfunctional. There's a lot of manipulation of information, keeping people in the dark, centralized decision-making, quashing of any contrary opinions, and so nobody's enjoying it. All the staff are living in fear. Freddy has been kicked out because he's perceived as a threat, since he will not submit to what is clearly wrong behavior. But because I'm the source of the ever-increasing funding, I'm actually helping to consolidate this very negative leadership model, which I really don't want to do. I'm kept sweet because I'm needed on side, whilst others are crushed. I feel like I want to quit and am looking into doing so, but I don't feel I have God's go-ahead to leave as yet. I'm praying and fasting and seeking the Lord.

Alongside all of this, I have some big missiological questions as well. Money is great, but it brings dependency and can create problems that didn't exist before. So to what extent am I just perpetuating that? I want to be a good role model for the next generation – sadly, it seems too late for this one.

I was invited to a VIP event for dinner in the Meridien Hotel. I went a little underdressed, but I struggle with these posh events anyway. Polite chit-chat is not my thing. Outside in the streets are loads of beggars and people dying; inside are a privileged hobnobbing elite stuffing their faces and cogitating over abstract concepts of peace and reconciliation. Actually, it was quite bizarre. I was sat with a pastor who is credited with a key role in the genocide, and yet has never publicly repented of it. Another church leader on our table, I know for a fact, has been bribing the immigration authorities to get some missionary friends kicked out of the country because the latter are exposing corruption within the organization. The list of dodgy "men of God" is a long one. I'm sick of Christians, but not of Christ!

I hate writing all this. I have become so cynical in such a short time. I recognize in myself how damaged and negative I'm becoming. I feel that any cutting edge I had has gone. I feel used. I feel disillusioned with most relationships and institutions. I'm sick of hypocrisy. My reactions are so feeble and ungodly. Come on, stand up and fight! Did I not expect times like this? Of course I did. So I can recognize Satan's work in all this, but at present don't have the energy or will to fight back.

I wrote to my dear Granny in Rwanda about the above concerns and her reply came when I needed it:

My dear Simon,

In your last prayer letter you spoke of wanting the mountains rather than the plains, in spite of the mists you meet there. I just feel you have walked into a mist which will soon clear, revealing the mountain – Jesus Himself. We have not seen our volcano, Muhabura, all the dry season because of the dusty heat haze, yet now in the rains we can see him again – but he was always there. I often think (and even preach) on Jesus being our Muhabura. The word means a landmark, literally the one who *habura* or un-loses us when we are *haba* or have lost our way. Muhabura is always there to help us get our bearings again.

My next observation on your email is colored by the teaching of the East African Revival of the 1930s and 1940s. We were told never to leave the church where we were called unless we were chucked out, the argument being that if we left, how could the Revival message get to that church? Simeon Nsibambi, one of God's key instruments at that time in Uganda, prayed and wept for years for Kampala Cathedral during the dismal lifeless services there until Revival came.

But the second thing we were told to pray for was a colleague with whom we could be a team of two, which others could join and with whom we could pray, however difficult the circumstances. God is still saying, "It is not good for man to be alone." In your case, the right wife for you is a prayer priority, but also a true brother-in-the-Lord as you had in Freddy.

I'm surprised you thought of leaving SU. Your calling was so clear to go there and you said your relationship with the tricky character was so much better. I read the letter to Titus this morning. How awful the Cretans were, but Titus was not told to leave them. Someone commenting about the East African Revival said that it was the first time that the Rwandans were seen to be free from lies and hypocrisy and it proved to be very attractive even to outsiders. But it was the Holy Spirit who did it. Pray that He does it again.

Don't make any irrevocable decision while you are in the mist – you might fall down a precipice!

Much love and prayer from Granny.

Where to look?

24 December 2000

An encouraging airmail letter arrived from Great Aunt Rosemary with the following lines:

Look around, and be distressed;
Look within, and be depressed;
Look to Jesus, and be at rest.

That's very helpful. It's Christmas Eve. I've just preached to a bunch of youngsters about Christ: "God-in-flesh" Incarnate. What unfathomable love, that He should leave the comfort and security of heaven to get His hands and feet dirty on this God-rejecting planet! What awesome news! I will be preaching up-country tomorrow, near where I was a few months back when the rebels were just round the corner and chose to leave me alone. Things are meant to hot up over the Christmas period, and we have been told by the embassy to stay in the capital. But if we always did as we were told, we'd not do very much at all. I can't imagine the early disciples consulting/adhering to the dictates of the respectable, politically correct local authorities of their day before setting out to storm the gates of hell as they preached the gospel. So, within reason, we've got to take risks. Actually, I think following Jesus was probably meant to be a risky business.

The Lord has continued to protect all of us along dangerous roads over the last few months. I had one particularly close shave when we broke down up-country, late in the day, after the army patrol had left the roads. In other words, the rebels were now in charge. It was nightfall, many had been killed recently in the area, and the truck had completely packed up. It's funny to look back and see how we still argued and haggled with a group of men before they were prepared, for a reasonable price ($20), to push us up to the crest of the hill so that we could then coast downhill for several miles to relative safety.

My boss, John, and several other dear friends narrowly missed being killed in an ambush last Friday as the rebels shot about twenty people dead in several cars. They wanted to show the International Donors' Conference in Paris that things weren't as stable as some were trying to suggest. $440 million in aid had just been agreed upon to help in the attempt to relaunch the economy, which is great news, provided the money goes to the right sources and isn't siphoned off along the way.

But the above might give a false impression of how undramatic the last few months have been. For me, they have been relatively inactive and therefore frustrating. If I'm honest, they have been my worst and hardest times since I left England back in 1998. We have had to cancel several evangelistic outings because of the security situation (see, I can be sensible too!), and I have had recurring bouts of amoebic dysentery. Certain relationships have been plain hard work. I have been extremely disillusioned by some high-profile church leaders. Life in general in Burundi, because of the extreme poverty and stressful situation, is very draining. So at times, when I was feeling really low, I wanted to pack my bags and go back home. And then I realized that here *is home*, so packing would be a waste of time! It's been tough.

Yet life being "tough" is all relative. Today Freddy came round with his wife, baby, and new addition to the family, Paul, to have an early Christmas celebration lunch with us. Freddy now once again lives by faith with no salary. Despite having virtually nothing himself, he recently came across Paul, lying in the sun, half-dead with malaria; and so he took him in as an unofficial second son. Paul has just had the best day of his life. This emaciated little boy stuffed his face next to me for an hour, never having seen so much food before. His story is that he recently watched his Mum and Dad die of tuberculosis in one of the refugee camps. His aunt then took him in, but he was constantly beaten, so he fled with his brother who subsequently got blown up by a grenade in the nearby market. That's where Freddy found him, lying in the shell of a burnt-out car – his new "home".

After our feast, I put him on a swing in the garden and pushed him several times. He started giggling and then laughing in innocent abandon, exhibiting a beautiful, rotten-toothed smile spread from ear to ear. In front of everyone, I suddenly choked and nearly burst into tears. How could such a simple thing as a swing ride bring such unadulterated joy? What on earth do I mean in the above paragraph when I say that my life has been "tough"? I have much to learn. Freddy and I praised God for Paul, as we saw his life as an illustration of grace. He has gone from being plucked out of the gutter to feasting like a king, adopted into a new and loving family.

I returned last week from three weeks' preaching in the USA. I met lots of wonderful, hospitable people and thoroughly enjoyed it. But the contrast with Burundi was hard to reconcile. Traveling between the two, via the UK, has been a culture shock both ways. We live on the same planet, yet most of us don't seem to really care enough for the hundreds of thousands of dying Pauls (who are not a statistic to God, even if they are to us) to be prepared to make any significant lifestyle sacrifices. We invest so much of our time, energy and resources in things of no eternal consequence and fall for the sucker lies of the evil one that possessions and status are the means to fulfillment and self-worth. It is so terribly insidious and subtle. Having said that, I did meet a number of middle-class people who were itching to live radical lives for Jesus, which always excites me, because it's so much easier to give up all you have when you haven't got much (like me!). It is much harder when you have plenty to give up and are clinging on to societal acceptance and respectability. Hence my burden to work with young people, so that early on in life they can establish the pattern of getting logically excited about evangelism and discipleship (i.e. building the kingdom) rather than disproportionately excited about a new carpet fitting or extension on the house (i.e. building bigger barns, as in Luke 12).

I don't want to appear harsh or ungracious – I'm just constantly trying to work through these issues in extreme circumstances and am more convinced by the day that the whole world is a sick place and things aren't getting any better. I'm becoming noticeably more cynical. So perhaps a year's study from September at Allnations near London will be good for me, getting out of the heat for a bit, to be spiritually refreshed, de-cynicalized and re-envisioned. People I trust are leaning on me, saying I'm a classic case for potential burn out. Hmm...

Back to tomorrow: assuming I do arrive back safely for lunch, we are then taking around 150 street kids for a party on the beach, sharing the tangible love of Jesus, being His hands and His feet, which is what each and every one of us is called to be. So here's to a blessed, happy and meaningful Christmas – not looking around and getting distressed, nor looking within and being depressed, but, *praise God*, looking to Jesus and experiencing His wonderful rest. I can't wait!

5

A Sense of Urgency

I have been impressed with the urgency of doing. Knowing is not
enough; we must apply. Being willing is not enough; we must do.

Leonardo da Vinci

Fatalities and fruit
23 January 2001

A few days ago an English person was shot dead. I was
actually preaching in the bush up in Rwanda at the time at a
youth event. I heard the news on the radio that a Brit had died
and presumed, because there are so few of us, that it was one
of my dear friends at Tearfund. I was far from any telephone
or Internet access so had to wait a while, heart in turmoil, to
hear who the unfortunate person was. As information trickled
out, we discovered it was a volunteer lady from Rwanda along
with her Burundian fiancé who were heading down to visit
his family, going against her organization's directives. I'm
gutted for them. But twenty other people were shot in the head
alongside her. This only made international news because a
white person died, which really annoys me. I'd traveled that

same route the day before with a friend, Audace, and he was also caught in the ambush. For whatever reason, however, he was one of four survivors who were stripped naked and told to flee. You can be sure he now wants to make his life count. By the time I got back to my emails, I found a number of people had written to see if I was the one who'd been killed. To reassure them and get some more prayer backup, I wrote the following:

I thought I would just share some of my recent diary with you. Hopefully it will help you to visualize what we get up to. Before that, on the prayer front, please pray for wisdom in discussing my future at SU. I see my role developing to include other groups and there are various issues that need addressing. Also, my TV-presenter cousin and a freelance cameraman just came out to do some filming for a potential documentary on my work out here. I'd appreciate prayers that the Lord would really use that. The impact could be deep, or nothing could come of it.

Anyway, here goes with the diary of the last few days:

19th January: For some reason I am thinking even more about death than usual. Is it paranoia? Is it the Holy Spirit telling me to be ready? Is tomorrow my last day? We joked with Paul the cameraman last week that the best way of making the documentary a huge hit, and thereby making his career, would be for me to die soon. It makes me feel like writing heavy letters to people. But then I get strangely superstitious, thinking along the lines that if I write them, then it is all the more likely to happen, which I know is a load of rubbish! So I was thinking of sitting down tonight and trying to prepare a great speech to be read out at my funeral to maximize the evangelistic opportunity that it would present. How macabre! No, I won't bother. I think I've already said to people what needs saying, although the prospect of death certainly makes you run through all your relationships so that you cannot be held accountable for not having been faithful in sharing the love of Christ with family, friends and colleagues, both in action and, more explicitly, in words. I don't want to seem obsessed with it, but there is no doubt that imminent death is a helpful focus in making an assessment of what really matters. How many people back home could do with a similarly enforced sense of urgency…

20th January: I just really felt the need for prayer cover over this weekend, so I emailed several groups to ask them to stand with us in intercession. We left for our weekend trip in three cars, the African Revival Ministries people and Cossette and I from SU. It felt like luxury, being in a car in which you actually expected to arrive the other end without a breakdown! It's such a beautiful drive through the mountains and there was no sign of trouble on the roads.

We arrived late, so went straight to the prison. We entered and were ushered past hundreds of criminals into a room maybe 60 feet by 45 feet. They could so easily have done anything to us if they'd wanted to. Once we were inside, the prisoners then squeezed in like sardines until there were, I guess, 350 people inside this cramped space and another 50 at the windows, listening intently. The spiritual atmosphere was naturally heavy, but the band started playing and the heaviness visibly and tangibly lifted as we worshipped the Lord. I preached from 1 Peter 2:22–25 on Christ's substitution on the cross to make us free – yes, free even in prison – shouting rather than speaking because of the commotion caused by more and more people constantly trying to push themselves within sight or earshot. We were sweating heavily in the suffocating heat and claustrophobia of such confines. Then Claver preached. These prisoners are considered the refuse of the world, the lowest of the low, and they know it, so they are prime candidates for accepting the message of God's grace. The response was huge. It was so precious, especially as this was the first time any group had been allowed into the prison to minister.

The evening meeting at the Lycée don Bosco, where we showed a film last year, however, was very shoddy. We were late arriving and setting up the equipment, we hadn't prayed together, there were problems with the sound, niggles within the music group, and those speaking simply didn't connect with the boys. Afterwards, Cossette had a group of lads around her, and she was hitting them with the real meaty gospel. I think she's wonderful. These were the hard-core dissenters, eating out of the palm of her hand for fifteen minutes as she put them in their places and yet lovingly shared Jesus with them too.

21st January: I slept on the floor with two young lads I didn't know on the bed above me snoring away. It wasn't the best night. Come morning there was no water in the whole guest-house, so there was solidarity in our smelliness! I was also seemingly the only one to bring toothpaste, so got my tube back virtually empty! I wasn't expecting to preach, but they asked me to when we arrived at the Eglise Vivante. We were there twice last year, so again most of them knew me and were delighted that we'd come back. It feels so nice to be up-country and still know so many people.

Early on in my preaching a lady to my left with her eyes shut started blurting out words incoherently. I wasn't sure whether this was demonic or not, but after waiting ten seconds, she continued being disruptive, so I went over to her, put my hand out and prayed over her out loud to be quiet in Jesus' name. She stopped immediately and I was able to continue. There was a really receptive atmosphere. I finished and sat down, but Claver reached over and nudged me, saying that he felt an appeal was necessary. I got back up and made a hard appeal. I said that God saw their hearts. He wasn't interested in lip service, hypocrisy or superficial mental acceptance and adherence to the theoretical validity of what they'd heard. "Only do it if you mean it," I urged them. "Get right with others in the congregation and then get right with God." Many chose to, and amongst those who came forward to respond was the previously disruptive lady. Amen! God knows the real fruit. I just know it was a privilege to be there.

We then prayed for the sick and lots of people came forward. So many people are dying of malaria at the moment. This beautiful little snotty-nosed eight-year-old came up to the front, gaunt, hunched, weak and sheepish. She was wearing a grubby pink jumper with a cute rabbit on it and the fast-fading words, which she no doubt didn't understand, "Will somebody give me a hug?" I wanted to hug the poor little thing to death. "Please heal her, Lord," I cried.

I needed to be back in the capital in two hours to preach there, so we hurried back, stopping off briefly at the side of the road to barter for a stick of bananas, which was our makeshift lunch. Further down the mountain road Cossette grabbed me and told me to stop urgently, as she was about to throw up. I slowed down, but then thought, "No way!" We couldn't stop there, of all roads in this country, let alone Africa and beyond! So she duly heaved out of the window and decorated the car's starboard side with some choice semi-digested banana! We did laugh – even she managed to. What a crazy life! I dropped off our belongings quickly at home. Nobody answered the door because Glorieuse's dad died last night, so although her role with her husband is to look after the property, they'd all gone up-country. Then we headed off to Kinama. The place was packed. I was ill-prepared and didn't preach well – I was plain exhausted and my delivery was flat. Finally, I made it home for a much-needed bath and bed.

22nd January: I slammed down lunch and headed to the Musaga Lycée. What a time! A whole load of scoffers saw me arrive and decided to stay and listen to the *muzungu* (white man). So, suddenly, instead of just having Christians, numbers were swelled by non-believers. I ditched my sermon and gave a straight evangelistic talk from Philippians 3:10–11. It was amazing. They were totally sullen and earnest, having begun so boisterously, and the Spirit was clearly at work. I said that they needed to take this seriously, as not one of them would have an excuse before God now that they had listened and heard the gospel clearly. "Who wants to know Christ?" I asked. About twenty stood and prayed with me. And they really prayed. I asked if I could come back next week and if they would bring their friends, and they all cheered enthusiastically. I can't wait! It was awesome. Wow! The opportunities for the gospel are all over the place. Surely we've got to maximize them. It is so clearly worth our absolute everything. God Almighty, thank you so much!

Emergency prayer, please!
26 February 2001

Things are not good at the moment (that is an understatement), so this is a rushed scribble and it will probably turn out to be jumbled and unordered, but the priority is to get people informed and praying. As I write this, I can hear gunshots. Many (no idea as yet how many) have been killed in the last two days. Various colleagues are hiding in different suburbs of the capital, afraid or forbidden to leave where they are. Things are extremely tense. Stray bullets are flying overhead. Thousands have fled their homes, even here in the capital, and are sat with their meager worldly possessions on the street corners, unsure what to do. A huge shell has just exploded a couple of miles away. We are listening to people dying. The whole experience is typically surreal and yet somehow typical of the way life is out here.

This is the situation that greeted me a few hours ago as I returned from another action-packed weekend up-country. People are surprised that we made it through. We drove down the hill and into Bujumbura, having heard that something was amiss, but not realizing how bad it was. The trashed houses were deserted and there was an eerie silence. There hadn't been any more soldiers than usual on the road, so it seemed, and we were in good spirits, having seen many come to the Lord over the last few days. More on that in a minute.

But why is it all happening right now? Well, the next round of peace talks in Arusha are under way. Those involved are seeking to elect a transitional leader, which is highly contentious. Mandela has had enough of being the peace-broker and looks like giving up, as it's all a bit too messy. He's trying to force things through, but the outlook is bleak.

Back to our weekend up-country. We left Saturday morning, having just received the news that two of our team narrowly escaped with their lives after skidding off the road and plunging thirty feet into a ravine. Apparently our truck may still be useable, but I'm not sure how. We arrived at Ibuye, which was badly hit in the war. I preached in the Cathedral. There were fourteen frocked pastors up by the altar, all but one with the regulation moustache, and with the Archbishop perched on his throne in the middle. As he pronounced a collect, a renegade goat waltzed in, nonchalantly evading a pastoral pincer movement before ducking behind the altar. I never saw it again – perhaps it was sacrificed or spontaneously combusted upon entering the Holy of Holies! I preached from Revelation 20 and knew that I had limited time. Towards the end of my sermon, one of the pastors from behind me came up and shook my hand, leaving a piece of paper in my palm, which I didn't bother reading, as I knew the gist of what it said already and I was drawing to a close anyway. I only read it when I sat back down. It read: "Time is money. *Il faut voir comment terminer* [one must see how to finish]"!

We also showed the *Jesus* film there after the service, before driving back to Ngozi and showing it in a packed church, where dozens responded to the call for salvation. I felt rough, but didn't really care, as this is such a joy to be a part of. During all of it, unbeknown to us, a battle was raging eighty miles away in Bujumbura, where I am now again.

Returning into Bujumbura, we sped past Kigobe, where the Johnsons live and work. Eleanor Johnson is eighty-six years young. Her husband, Carl, died a few weeks ago. They had been out here together for fifty-five years. Since yesterday, around 4,500 people have arrived on her compound – not something she needs as a recent widow who is grieving and trying to sort through years of her husband's accumulated paperwork, but people feel safe there.

When missionaries were getting kicked out in the 1980s, Carl just said, "God's not told me to go, so I'm staying." Their house became the heart of a refugee camp of thousands of people from 1993 onwards, as others fled whilst they chose to stay. It's a powerful witness.

At Carl's moving funeral, Eleanor said that in sixty and a half years of marriage, she had never heard him speak evil about anyone; and when his enemies spoke ill of him and she leapt to his defense, he would stop her in her tracks and say, "Dear, if you can't say anything nice about them, then just don't say anything at all." Wow!

Another old battler, same vintage year (1915), is Granny Guillebaud. I'll see her in two weeks when I drive up to Rwanda. She collapsed last week and her heart stopped beating, but she soon revived, declaring, "Well, God's obviously still got work for me to do!" These are tough acts to follow, but definitely also role models and examples for all of us to emulate with their zeal, passion, commitment and perseverance.

Last week, I had a bout of suspected malaria (it turned out to be food poisoning), which was utterly miserable when it kicked in. Come morning, after umpteen hot and cold sweats, and regular dashes to the lavatory, I got ready to go to the doctor. Not only was there no electricity, but there was also no water for the first time in ages. In my feeble, dazed state, I tried to prepare a stool sample (why is it called that?). To my horror, I discovered I hadn't taken the lid off the container, so it went everywhere, including all over my hands, and there was no water to wash it off with! What a mess! I fumbled around barefoot in the dark and failed to see a glass bottle on the floor, so I kicked it and it shattered. Glass shards went everywhere. Disaster! Well, yes, I did manage to see the funny side, eventually.

Perhaps it seems trite of me to lighten the tone when things are in such a desperately serious state around me. Well, without a sense of humor, it would be hard to get by in these extremes. Not many people will be laughing in Burundi tonight, though. Most people's "disasters" are much more serious than mine. The malaria epidemic continues, as does famine in many parts of the country. Some eat bark or leaves just to stop their stomachs rumbling and to appease the pangs of hunger. Fear is in the air. So is despair. What will happen in the coming days?

Senseless killing
28 February 2001

News continues to arrive all the time. The juxtaposition of routine normality and sheer hell-on-earth is hard to reconcile. Nathan is trying to get his cousin's body back, which has been lying rotting on the ground in one of the rebel-held parts of town since Saturday. If they try to go anywhere near it, they get shot at. And hidden somewhere in one of the shelled houses is the dead man's young wife and two-month-old baby. She probably knows she will never see her husband again. Perhaps she's just waiting for the finality of the dreaded news to be brought to her. She's the last of her own family – all her relatives were killed in 1993. Apparently, her husband was a lovely young man, although he didn't profess to know Jesus. So do I have to believe he has gone to hell? That he is facing a Christless eternity? That "God's wrath remains on him" (John 3:36)? That he has been "punished with everlasting destruction" (2 Thessalonians 1:9)? Well, do I? I don't want to. But is it the truth? Do I really believe it? Then I must live more urgently.

On the news I saw a man talking about his family who had been hacked to death, thirteen of them in all, leaving just him and one daughter. I went to bed. I had a tape playing quietly, to send me to sleep as usual, and then it started. Gunfire and shells both sound very different to what you'd imagine. Whereas for most of the year it has been a matter of several miles away, now it was just a matter of hundreds of yards. We'd had popcorn at my friend Julie's – this wasn't a dissimilar sound – and then came deep, reverberating thuds. Helge rang from next door. We all sat in the dark in the corridor between thick walls, just with a candle. It went on for half an hour or so. Such is life here. We trust God to get us through each day.

6

THE ADVENTURE OF LIVING OR THE SAFETY OF EXISTING

There are those who like to say "yes" and there are those who prefer to say "no". Those who say "yes" are rewarded by the adventures they have; those who say "no" are rewarded by the safety they attain.

Keith Johnson

Protection money
1 March 2001

My current housemates at the guest house, Regine (German) and Regula (Swiss), went off up-country. They have received a letter from the local rebel group asking them for their license plates so that they don't get ambushed, and for a "contribution" to the cause (i.e. protection money). But these terrific ladies refuse to cooperate. We prayed for them and expected them to get through, but talked openly about the fact that they might die en route. Nevertheless, they weren't going to allow intimidation to keep them in Bujumbura as slaves to fear, unable to function effectively. They do their nations proud.

Recently, a bullet pinged into the wall, narrowly missing my friend Sarai. She's a special woman: a single mum, she has taken fifteen orphans into her household. She doesn't even have a fixed income. "Simon, God just sends them to me – how can I turn them away?" she told me. "When there is no food on the table at breakfast, I don't worry at all. I've been obedient and done my bit – God has to be faithful and provide!" I love her reasoning: "You know, Simon, everyone has problems. If you have kids, you have problems; if you don't have any kids, you still have problems. So you might as well have kids and have problems, as they also bring joy!"

The rising tide of AIDS
2 March 2001

I went to morning prayers at our SU offices. As usual, the person opening in prayer said, *"Imana yacu, turagushimiye kuko watuzigamiye kugez' uyu musi"* ("Our God, we thank you for protecting us until today"). Then as we started to read from the Bible, there was shooting in the hills and people began fleeing. Many friends have been affected by this. A grenade exploded in Sylvestre's bedroom, but fortunately he was in the next room at the time. Pastor Tharcisse from one of the outer suburbs rang up and said that they had had to flee their home. He and his wife had nothing except the clothes they were wearing. Nothing in the world! At night, she washed her dress, he washed his trousers and shirt, and they left them hanging to dry in the hovel they were squatting in, putting their clothes back on still wet the next morning. So he was asking if I had a shirt and a pair of trousers to spare. My colleague Evariste said to me, "We are waiting to die, my whole family. Can you take just one of my children in your luggage back to England so that at least one of us survives?" I couldn't tell whether he was joking or not. John's nephew was also amongst those killed.

Some non-governmental organizations (NGOs) evacuated to Kenya, but most didn't. We slipped across Lake Tanganyika into Eastern Congo for some very productive times with church leaders, doing AIDS sensitization from a Christian perspective, trying to break the taboo and get the church to face up to the reality of this disaster. There is so much ignorance concerning the disease, like the satanic myth that you can get rid of AIDS if you sleep with a virgin, which leads to many infected men raping baby girls. Incidence of HIV+/AIDS has gone up a staggering 10 per cent in two years, mainly because of the serial raping taking place because of the prevailing lawlessness. Today's 15-year-old boy has a 35 per cent chance (more than 1 in 3) of contracting and dying of AIDS in the next 15 years. How horrifying is that?

God is faithful
4 April 2001

I constantly feel the need for more prayer backup, so I wrote to friends recently with the following:

How are things? I hope that all is well your end – that you are enjoying the adventure of living rather than the safety of existing, that you are getting excited by and investing in the eternal rather than the temporal, and that you are aspiring to being biblically obedient rather than just biblically literate.

I am currently in the rolling hills of the North of Burundi, at our biggest youth camp to date. My tent is pitched on a classroom floor next to a latrine which has overflowed, so it smells a bit! But at least it is flat and dry and I wake up to the awesome view of the sun rising above the dense early-morning mist nestling in the valley below. There are about 350 of us here for five days and it is extremely tiring, because these youth are so thirsty for God's Word. This morning at 6.40 a.m. I felt quite pious and holy as I went up early to the meeting-room to pray and set a good example for the kids, only to hear and realize from a distance that I was far from being one of the first. About fifty were already praying and crying out to the Lord in earnest. I guess things are so obviously desperate here that we know we need to be praying. Poor old beautiful Burundi!

Things have been challenging since I last wrote. Over 50,000 people fled their homes in the capital itself. Many were killed. In fact, last week they discovered a mass grave of 200 bodies in Kinama, just a couple of miles away, at a site where I regularly preach. An 8 p.m. curfew was put in place and every night we listened to the sounds of shelling and shooting, knowing that lives were being lost at a steady rate.

In the meantime, I retained the not-so-prestigious Burundi Squash Championship. As always, the two worlds I mix in are hard to reconcile. I then preached in Rwanda and Uganda either side of a week's break away from the draining stress of Burundi. The highlight was a near-death experience of a different kind as I went white-water rafting with some mates on the Nile and half-drowned on the last rapid, a notorious stretch creatively named "the Bad Place"! Bouts of dysentery and flu have taken turns in pestering me over the last month, but I am still on good form.

An American called Chuck Baldwin, representing a ministry called Evangelism Explosion, came and introduced the work to a group of missionaries a while ago to see if anyone would get excited about launching it in the country. I saw EE's potential, so have taken it on and believe it can and will have a massive role in equipping the church in evangelism and discipleship. He came to deliver the first EE clinic, which went very well, and certainly lived up to its name – fighting and shelling kicked in loudly just as we began! Many came to the Lord and the others shared my excitement at the potential of EE to transform churches. It's got some significant weaknesses as an approach, but in general is a brilliant tool for both evangelism and discipleship. During the week I was falsely and randomly accused of singing at 3 a.m. – very bizarre! As a result I had to go to the police station on three different days and they wanted to keep me in prison (of course, they really wanted a bribe). All this was happening as I was trying to act as main facilitator for the intensive EE training of pastors. It was blatant opposition by the evil one and we were able to rejoice and press on anyway. On one visit it looked like the authorities weren't going to release me. It was all a pack of lies, but I was fined $20, and then I discovered that it was a case of mistaken identity. They thought I was someone else!

The atmosphere here overall is very heavy. *But God is faithful* and it's such a privilege to do life with some incredible people who say "yes" to God's call to obedience and thereby embrace the adventure of living. May I never end up saying "no" and settling for the safety of existing!

Health clinic attacked
12 April 2001

I wonder if we are on the edge of genocide. I spoke to my housemate Regine, who had had an "interesting" day: the local rebel leaders showed up and asked her what on earth she was still doing there, because the rebels were on the next hill. All the cars heading for Gitega were stopped at Muramvia, as there was a battle under way. The Government claims it killed sixty-four rebels. They're apparently making their way up from Tanzania to regroup in the Kibira forest in preparation for a huge onslaught. If they were united, they would have a chance of winning, but there's no unity with them either.

Regine rang again to say that it was all action around her. But when I tried to assume the role of Captain Sensible and suggest that she should stick in the capital for a couple of weeks until it calms down, she replied that the people around her didn't have the choice to leave, so why should she? I then bumped into my death-threat messenger man, Aloise, and that always stirs the old adrenaline a bit.

An hour later there came the instantly recognizable, pathetic tootle of a horn from behind the gate. It was Regine back from Muramvia. She had had two minutes to decide whether to pack and leave, or stay and risk getting raped and killed. Someone rang her and said that the rebels were 3 km away, and then the battle began. As she left, there were streams of people along the roads clutching bundles of their worldly possessions and with their animals in tow.

And now as I write this, the local school and church are burning, just 1 km from the health center. All are fleeing, hiding in the church, and Claver (her Burundian colleague) is opening up all the stores so that the rebels can pillage everything but hopefully won't kill anyone. Regine is receiving this news on the phone next to me as I write – she has just put it down and naturally burst into tears, feeling guilty that she left, although it was clearly the right thing to do.

We await more news. Sometimes it feels like we're living in a dream. The general feeling is of tense anticipation and almost excitement, as if the big day is about to arrive, but nobody knowing how big and bad it will be.

I received this email from the UN:

Rebels reportedly planning huge offensive against Bujumbura
– informed sources in Bujumbura have warned of preparations

for a vast rebel offensive against the Burundian capital… An estimated 10,000 rebels are poised to enter Burundi, in addition to some 8,000 already in the country.

Tears to cry
13 April 2001

Regine got a call at 4 a.m. from Claver. He just wanted to be comforted. Everyone was sheltering in the church next door or had fled. The health clinic had not been burnt (we found out later that it was the only health clinic not to have been trashed by the rebels as they swept up from the South). He relayed lots more dreadful news – all the houses are burning; lots of dead cattle are strewn about the place; cars have been set alight; there was an aerial bombardment by the army; all the people have fled or are in hiding. The consequence is that within a week, when the dust has settled, the whole area will be back to square one. How utterly senseless!

Ernest and Glorieuse's families are somewhere in the midst of all this carnage, and although they are worried, Glorieuse simply laughed and said that was just the way it was in Burundi – people are always dying, so there was no point crying. Regine retorted that God gave us tears to cry. She's truly devastated and it's sobering knowing how close she was to being caught up in it, having been there just yesterday.

We've been warned to have bags packed and ready, but I hope I would choose to stay at almost any cost (unless trusted local friends told me to go, as I was jeopardizing their safety). I should really begin stock-piling fuel and foodstuffs. It doesn't sink in, though, quite how serious things are. My friend Mary, who lives a few streets away, just arrived this evening to find her guard shell-shocked, as he comes from Muramvia. He'd received the news that his house had been completely razed to the ground. He's about to get married and had invested all the money he'd ever saved to build it. Now it's gone – one of many such cases – it's all so futile.

Morbid fatalism
15 April 2001

It's Easter Sunday! I heard early morning shooting and wondered whether it would really kick in this time. It only went on for ten minutes. As I spent time with the Lord after sunrise, I watched a bird painstakingly yet faithfully building its nest in the tree above me. It seemed a picture of so many people in the land, like Mary's unfortunate guard, who are trying to (re)build their lives, working hard at it, yet what is the point when within a few weeks/months/years it all goes up in smoke again? I'm not sure what we should still be praying for any more. Does God definitely want there to *not* be a war? Because without full-blown war, the situation will go on interminably. With war, at least sweeping changes and radical reforms can be made. Nobody's wishing for a situation like Rwanda to reoccur, but at least they are now rebuilding there. Whereas with the *status quo* here, only about 5,000 out of the population of 8 million are the winners.

I got an email from my sister Tracy telling me that she loved me, that she didn't want me to die, that I should be careful etc. It made me want to cry! The situation is so strange. I am waiting for bloody carnage. Yet, I cannot stir up the emotions appropriate for such an extreme scenario. I should feel frightened, excited, tense, paranoid. But I'm plain bored. I felt like crying just now out of bored restlessness and the grim realization that tens of thousands of lives are about to be ruined. *Ni ko bimeze*, as they say out here, or *c'est comme ça* – "that's just the way it is". Away with such morbid fatalism!

Scantily clad temptation
26 April 2001

In the midst of all the stress, I attended a Belgian embassy function. Kate was there, representing the UN, and she looked gorgeous in a figure-hugging scarlet outfit. Afterwards, she invited me round to her apartment for a catch-up chat. I went back home to make a few calls first and then headed to her place in the Quartier Asiatique. This is humbling to write, but I was dangerously near to stumbling. Out of nowhere, I suddenly wanted her so much. We sat on the same sofa and I found her tanned, shapely body almost irresistible. There was so much for both of us to lose. I think each was waiting for a blatant enough sign from the other. A fierce battle was raging within me. My heart was beating so fast that my voice trembled. "Hold back, Simon, behave yourself!" "No way, come on, what a great opportunity!" It was five minutes to the curfew. Was I going to stay the night? I so badly wanted to. But I knew I had to get out and go home. I pecked her hurriedly on the cheek to say goodbye and, thankfully, didn't linger. I thought I was going to explode in frustration when I got home. I felt drained of energy, dizzy and breathless. I was disappointed that I hadn't gone for it, further disappointed that I had considered going for it, but in all honesty regretting that my faith and conscience wouldn't allow me to follow my natural, carnal instincts. I don't think I've ever experienced such strength of emotion. It's underlined to me the fact that maybe I really do need a wife. But who would be willing to live this kind of life?!

Are you ready?

17 May 2001

Last Sunday, just before leaving Burundi to make a visit to the UK, I preached in a vibrant church in a slum near the Congolese border called Gatumba. The message from the parable of the ten virgins in Matthew 25 was:

1. Jesus is coming.
2. No one knows when.
3. So are you ready?

Many repented and came to Christ. Two days later, I was on my motorbike going in that same direction when I was stopped by soldiers and ordered to return to the capital: "Come back later. They're fighting up ahead in Gatumba." Rebels had moved across the border and were attacking the army. Many died. God knows how many it was, but it made me think: were those who died ready? Am I? Are we living with a sense of urgency, as if we believe the gospel is the absolute truth for absolutely everybody?

Now it's 11.54 a.m., pouring with rain, and my car's just broken down on the way out of Cambridge. I'm typing this as I wait for the breakdown man to come and help me out. It's a far cry from Burundi: last time I broke down was in rebel-held territory at dusk south of the capital, Bujumbura, but out there I couldn't just dial on a phone and have someone show up promptly to sort things out. It was a narrow escape – one of many over the last few years – and I feel relieved to be back in England for a while. I returned two days ago and have just finished my second of dozens of preaching engagements in the UK over the next few months.

Things have been tough and tense over the last couple of months. I was wrong in my prediction of when the all-out assault would begin, but it is still expected imminently.

So I'm now back in the UK for a few months' preaching at least, and maybe will stay for a year studying at Allnations. I'm still praying for guidance on that one. My health for the last few months has been terrible, so perhaps a year back in the UK is what the doctor ordered. Last Friday, we had a farewell reunion at SU in which we looked back at what had been achieved in the last two and a half years. It was amazing. We have been involved in more evangelism in more schools and churches than any other group, seeing several thousand come to the Lord. We're pioneering a Christian approach to the AIDS epidemic, the children's ministry is growing, which is so important with such a young population, and there's a whole lot more. Praise the Lord! He's protected us through many hazardous journeys. One SU volunteer was shot dead last year, but nobody died in three serious car crashes – twice when the cars rolled over a few times, and once when the truck plummeted down a ravine. It has been a wild ride.

7

LESSONS FROM THE CONFLICT

Everyone dreams, but not equally. Those who dream by night in the dusty recesses of their minds wake up in the day to find it was vanity. But the dreamers of the day are dangerous people, for they may act out their dreams with open eyes to make it happen.

Lawrence of Arabia

Dreamers of the Day
20 August 2001

Dear Dreamers of the Day,

Greetings from the South of France, where I have just arrived for our family holiday. In the three months since the last prayer letter, I have preached on around ninety occasions around the UK. I've had some powerful and fruitful times, but also some very tiring ones, so I figured a break was in order. Yesterday, I jumped fifty feet from a cliff edge into the river below and now feel slightly bruised as a result! But it was an awesome sensation stepping out into nothing and sailing through the air! The weather here is perfect, the landscapes are stunning, we are feasting like kings, enjoying each other's company and, in the words of Louis Armstrong's song, I say to myself, "What a wonderful world"!

Yes, it is wonderful and yes, when I creep out in the early morning light to pray before the others wake up, I do praise the Lord for His creative power and extravagance, as well as His goodness, faithfulness and mercy. But as I worship, I also picture the browbeaten and disheveled mother across the lake from me in the Congo. She has been raped by soldiers on her way to and from work almost every day for the last six years, as she valiantly seeks to provide for her destitute children. So I ask myself: "Is it really such a wonderful world?"

I have before me a document entitled: "Indonesia 2000 – Genocide of a Christian Minority", which contains gruesome tales of murder, rape and torture, carried out by Islamic fundamentalist Jihad warriors on thousands of innocent people. Their crime? Saying, "Jesus is Lord." I'm also reading a detailed account of Rwanda's genocide – not the most cheerful reading either. In fact, that's surely not the kind of reading for a holiday? But yes, it is exactly the kind of reading I need, because I'm in precious little danger of not having a wonderful time in this idyllic environment, whilst in huge danger of being so comfortable and settled that I become oblivious to the battle at hand. I've just read the following by John Piper in his book, *Let the Nations be Glad*:

> Most people show by their priorities and casual approaches
> to spiritual things that they believe we are in peace, not in
> wartime… In wartime we are on the alert. We are armed. We are
> vigilant. In wartime we spend money differently, because there
> are more strategic ways to maximize our resources. The war effort
> touches everybody. We all cut back. The luxury liner becomes
> a troop carrier… Who considers that the casualties of this war

do not merely lose an arm or an eye or an earthly life, but lose everything, even their own soul, and enter a hell of everlasting torment?

So, I enjoy the holiday, but I can't deceive myself into thinking that the war is on hold. People are dying in ignorance all around us and thereafter facing a Christless eternity. We're still soldiers and there's no room for complacency – hence the early morning prayer warfare before the others surface.

Piper goes on:

> Probably the number one reason why prayer malfunctions in the hands of believers is that we try to turn a wartime walkie-talkie into a domestic intercom. Until you know that life is war, you cannot know what prayer is for... But what have millions of Christians done? We have stopped believing that we are in a war. No urgency, no watching, no vigilance. No strategic planning. Just easy peace and prosperity. And what did we do with the walkie-talkie? We tried to rig it up as an intercom in our houses – not to call in firepower for conflict with a mortal enemy, but to ask for more comforts in the den...

Having lived in Burundi's war zone for the last three years and experienced the imminence of death, listened to the shelling, seen the devastation, grieved for the departed, it was very much easier for me to live urgently there, than it is now that I am back in the UK for a year. But that is the challenge for all of us who are privileged enough to live in more apparently "functional" and stable societies. So where is the urgency in our churches? Where is my own sense of urgency to reach out to a sophisticated and respectable but dying world? It's dirty work. It's unglamorous. It's costly. It's painful. And I wonder how many of us are striving to maintain or create our own "wonderful worlds" this side of eternity, when actually the

Bible's model of authentic Christian living is far removed from our own. The New Testament believers understood that they were "strangers in the world" (1 Peter 1:1) and therefore lived in the light of eternity. Similarly, our brothers and sisters in Indonesia, China, Pakistan, Laos etc., who are being tortured/raped/imprisoned/killed as I write and you read this, know more clearly and cling to the fact more dearly that absolute truth is worth absolute sacrifice – with multiple promises from the Lord that, for example, they are blessed in persevering under trial, because when they have stood the test, they will receive the crown of life that God has promised to those who love Him (James 1:12).

Excuse the digression – this was meant to be a prayer letter about the Congo and Burundi! I'm afraid Congo is possibly the worst place on the planet at the moment. Urgent prayers are needed. Here's an extract from my diary:

10th July: I've just seen a news report on the TV about the Congo which has reduced me to tears. I feel crushed. Two and a half million people have died in the last couple of years as a result of the war, famine and disease. [By 2010 the number had risen to 5.4 million, according to the UN.] What a mammoth statistic! I can't get my head around it. I knew just one of that huge number: Rangi's cute little baby – the poor thing only lasted four months. *But it wasn't a "thing", for Christ's sake!* And neither is that number just a statistic to God, even if it is to us. How He must weep. Come, Lord Jesus!

Burundi is as near to finding a peaceful solution as it has been for some time, whilst remaining as near to potential genocide as ever. I think at last even the most stubborn elements are tiring of war and longing for peace. It has been agreed to have two eighteen-month periods in office as a transition to free elections again, the first one with a Tutsi in charge (the current President, Buyoya), and the second with a Hutu, Domitien Ndayizeye. Meanwhile, indiscriminate killings continue. Since I left, a friend's driver was shot dead and two diocesan staff were also murdered. Our SU team was stopped by rebels, but mercifully allowed to pass through the area unharmed. My colleague, Evariste, was attacked in the night, but his family got away without being killed.

Anticipating burn out, I have begrudgingly accepted that I need to take a year out from Burundi, so I will be studying at Allnations, just north of London, and preaching at weekends all round the country. It's a brilliant place, but my heart remains with my brothers and sisters in Burundi and I will return as soon as possible.

So, Dreamers of the Day, God bless you all, and don't stop dreaming. Let's be dangerous people all the way until we graduate. Then it will be undeniably, eternally, truly, wonderful. Keep your eyes open all the way!

A life well lived
12 September 2001

Supergranny Guillebaud has just graduated to glory in Rwanda, aged eighty-six! Three years earlier, once Grandpa had died in England, she had promptly declared, "I'm going back to Rwanda!" As a widow she had her work cut out because the genocide had left literally tens of thousands of widows in her area. But she duly went out to live with Auntie Meg in the North at a place called Byumba and started a widows' meeting. The first week there were 30 in attendance, then 80, then 100, and it steadily grew to 400 before they had to split into groups because they'd grown so large.

Three years later, on her last day in action, she preached energetically for an hour in her widows' meeting. Then for some reason she said goodbye to them (as if she knew she was homeward bound). She had the last photo of her alive taken as she danced with the widows before the Lord, and then she returned home for a game of Scrabble. She had a stroke in the night and died peacefully today.

What a woman of God! What a challenge! To me, her complete surrender in every aspect of her life was an absolutely logical outworking of the realization that heaven is our home, not here. So come on, where is the next generation? Here I am, send me! I want to be part of it. Count me in! Let's seek God's face and not settle until we know the answer to the question: Where do I fit into His plan? And let's make sure He is not relegated to fitting into my/our plans.

Life lessons from the Burundian bloodshed
8 October 2001

Allnations is a great place to be. I have a year to sharpen my theology of mission, to bounce ideas off people with much more experience than myself, to assess where I might have gone wrong and could improve in the future, and to process an extraordinary few years in a calmer and safer environment. There are students from twenty-four different nations and it is a rich experience. Emmanuel and Asele, dear friends from Burundi, are here, and there is another Burundian called Theo. I don't doubt that in future years the Lord will use us together in ministry for His glory, although at this stage we cannot see what that will look like. Theo's story is a remarkable one:

At the end of 1993, tens of thousands of Burundians were being murdered on both sides of the tribal divide as genocide kicked in following the assassination of the Hutu President. As a Hutu, Theo had to flee, or otherwise he would have been killed by the Tutsi. He walked several hundred miles through the bush into Tanzania. On the way he had a number of extraordinary escapes.

At one stage he was taken by a blood-crazed gang of Hutus, who insisted that he and his five friends kill some Tutsis to prove they were Hutus. Theo was the leader of the Christian Union at school and the other five looked to him. The choice was basically to kill or be killed. He chose to be killed. He was forced to lie down on the floor, where he prayed a feeble prayer of resignation and waited for the machete to land on his neck. But suddenly a military helicopter flew overhead and everyone dispersed in different directions, so Theo and his friends continued their journey.

Further on, as they crossed a tarmac road, a military tank spotted them and sprayed them with bullets. As they fled, many were mown down, but again Theo survived and continued making his way through the bush. Later he and his group found themselves surrounded by a Tutsi mob. Their end had surely come. There was no escape. But suddenly a Tutsi girl he had once helped with a work assignment at school years before ran up to him and jumped into his arms. "If you want to kill him, you'll have to kill me first!" she cried. Her brother was influential in the army, so the murderers let him go.

Once in Tanzania, thousands of Hutu refugees were dying of dysentery. Theo lay down to die, questioning why God would have spared him so much only for him to die now, without even having had the opportunity to testify to God's glory. Suddenly a white man drove up in a truck, lugged him and a few others into the back, and took them to a hospital. One of them died on the way. Theo was given medicine before being dumped back in the bush. That was enough to save him. Some time later, a female Swiss doctor found him and gave him a job, training him up as a nurse.

As the refugee camps became more established, all young men were being forced to join the rebel Hutu movement, but Theo didn't want to, so he fled to Kenya with some others.

He was caught by the Kenyan authorities and was going to be deported when a mystery woman (most likely a prostitute, from her manner), for whatever reason, came to their aid, going to the immigration officer who was about to sentence them to deportation and imprisonment, and arranging for him to release them. They were whisked off to the officer's house, given clothes, food, a chance to wash, and false Tanzanian papers enabling them to get into Kenya and apply for asylum.

Theo's remarkable journey continued as a missionary he hardly knew sent off an email on his behalf, and Theo was able to go to Bible college, first in Kenya, and now at Allnations in England.

That concise summary doesn't do justice to Theo's whole story, but during the time I spent with him, he raised some issues from his experiences which profoundly challenged me:

1. He said that God's faithfulness does not depend on man's faithfulness. As he lay there waiting to have his head chopped off, he said his prayer was utterly faithless. But God, in His grace, had mercy.

2. He had a wholly inadequate grasp of what constitutes salvation. He'd been taught that you come to Jesus to be saved from hellfire and to get a ticket to heaven. But he wasn't equipped to live on earth. We don't just believe in life after death, but life to the full before death, and a fuller understanding of salvation equips us to engage on both levels more effectively.

3. There was the time when he was languishing in the Tanzanian refugee camp. He was angry at everyone – the other tribe for killing his tribesmen, the international community for not helping them fast enough, the manipulation of politicians etc. People were dying all

around him and his greatest anger was directed at the church. "Where is the church?" he asked himself. Islam spread fast in the refugee camps because Muslims were there providing emergency relief and sharing their things, whilst the Tanzanian churches stayed away. Many converted to Islam purely because they said, "The Muslims are the ones who love us." However, as his anger boiled over at God, he heard the Lord reply, "*You are the church!*" And with that understanding, he got his hands dirty, mucked in, and shone as a beacon of light in the darkness to counteract the advance of Islam and all the evils being perpetrated in the camps.

4. He said, "Don't ever underestimate small acts of kindness" – the bits of food people gave him, the medicine, the mystery prostitute or the white man in the truck, the email sent to a faraway Bible college. Sometimes, looking at Africa, the problems can seem so overwhelming that we resist getting involved, but his story included lots of crucial little acts of kindness and intervention that kept him alive and led to him now being able to fulfill God's destiny and make a big impact on his nation.

5. His legitimate and deep-seated prejudice against Tutsi was profoundly rocked by that young lady risking her life to save his. She was prepared to die for him. No longer could he lump all Tutsis together as evil people. There were good and bad amongst both Hutu and Tutsi.

I am humbled by his story on many levels, and it makes me want to learn these key life lessons:

1. Thank God that His faithfulness doesn't depend on mine! I will choose to live a life oozing grace and

gratitude for His intervention in my ongoing journey.

2. A full view of salvation includes life both before and after death. Is my own view defective or imbalanced? The stakes are high, so I want to give my all to seeing people saved for eternity, but also so that they fully engage in this life too.

3. When I'm tempted to get angry, despairing or frustrated about the church, when I next criticize or disparage her, may I stop seeing the problem as being "out there" and instead hear God's rallying cry: "*You* are the church!"

4. What small acts of kindness can I do today which, under God's sovereign hand, could lead to beautiful fruit in the future?

5. For me, my prejudices aren't so much towards Hutu or Tutsi, but I most certainly have them. We all do. And as followers of Jesus – an immigrant, a refugee, an outsider – we Christians have ironically had a very mixed track record in this area. So what is my attitude and how am I actively engaged in helping the foreigner, the outsider, the immigrant, the alien, the marginalized? Or is following Jesus about being a cosseted member in the safety of the "in-crowd"?

It's worth thinking about...

Chaotic cacophony
Christmas Day 2001

It's 6 a.m. and as the sun rises, hundreds of people are gathered along the shore of Lake Tanganyika to be baptized. Many others come along to share the moment. The atmosphere is buzzing on this joyous occasion. About a dozen churches are represented. But they are all in different groups, singing different songs, with different leaders. The result is an undignified chaotic cacophony and nobody seems to know what is happening or who is in charge. In short, it's a mess, and as a picture, it aptly reflects the state of the church in Burundi: there is a lot of fruit in these days of extreme suffering, but also a lack of unity within the body of Christ and a lack of clear godly leadership from the front.

Identified with His death
28 December 2001

I wanted to write an end-of-year missive to all our supporters:

How are things? It's been four months since the last prayer letter, so I thought I should update you. I am back in Burundi for the Christmas break, in order to keep up with what is going on in the office, as well as at a broader level. It's a joy to be back home, but things are very delicate. More on that in a moment. I have just been to visit a friend who was recently diagnosed with AIDS. She was lying in her hut, looked visibly more emaciated than before, and is dying. Her errant husband was murdered in the genocide in 1994, leaving her as a widow with three children to bring up, and now she too will die. So who will look after them? Yet another three to add to the mind-numbing statistic of AIDS orphans in Africa.

It simply re-emphasizes to me the priority of our Aid for AIDS project. But things are not looking good at the moment. There has been a breakdown in relationships within the leadership of SU and the project, and reconciliation needs to take place. I won't go into any more details, but please pray into this. The rest of the personnel have been affected and it is not overstating it to say that this could be make or break for SU as a whole. I myself am in a very difficult situation and can see no positive outcome.

The situation in the country as a whole hasn't changed much. The transitional government was implemented on 1 November and there are peacekeeping troops from South Africa here who don't seem to be doing a great deal apart from fuelling the trade in prostitution and therefore exacerbating the AIDS situation. At night there is the usual gunfire. I read a UN report yesterday saying that Government troops had killed 515 rebels recently outside the capital and lost 26 of their own, but who knows the real number. It is far from peaceful.

As one year ends and a new one begins, I cry out to God that my passion, and yours, will grow for the glory of His name. He is surely worth "our utmost for His highest". Oswald Chambers wrote the following:

> Get alone with Jesus and either tell Him that you do not want sin to die out in you; or else tell Him that at all costs you want to be identified with His death.

So, as we think about the coming year and conceivably make fresh resolutions, let's get alone with Him, put first things first, and then surely the rest will be added to us.

8

HOW HUNGRY ARE WE?

If you have to calculate what you are willing to give up for Jesus Christ, never say that you love Him. Jesus Christ asks us to give up the best we have got to Him, our right to ourselves.

Oswald Chambers

Calculations
24 April 2002

If what Oswald Chambers says is true, and I believe it is, then I wonder where we are at in our calculations?

I have just returned from seeing someone in hospital who "gave up the best she had", her right to herself. Great-aunt Rosemary Guillebaud is in a coma and may die any time now. But, like Super-granny Guillebaud, here is another amazing woman of God about to graduate to glory. She went out to Africa in 1925 and, amongst other things, over the ensuing decades translated the Bible into Kirundi. She has been used in the lives of literally hundreds of thousands of people. This makes it all the more sad to see her so feeble and frail, but what a reception awaits! I prayed with her in Kirundi, not knowing if she could hear, although she did open her eyes a couple of times. I choked a little as I thanked her for her example and vowed to continue in her footsteps in Burundi to see that nation transformed for Christ.

So how is Burundi? Well, I received a report via the UN today which catalogues all the problems and provides very few reasons for optimism. It says:

> Of all the negative factors which are destroying confidence in the whole Burundian peace process, the absence of a cessation of hostilities / ceasefire, the continuing absence of an inclusive ceasefire process and no prospect of an end to the war in sight, are by far the most dominant ones. This simply means that the whole Burundian peace process will collapse if the ceasefire process cannot soon produce a positive result. If the ceasefire process meetings being held in Pretoria, South Africa, do not show significant progress, there will be no alternative but to re-evaluate the whole ceasefire process.

The friend I wrote about last time who was sick with AIDS died a couple of months ago. As she lay on her deathbed, people who lived around the corner came and took her fence for firewood, knowing that she couldn't do anything about it. Now her three children are left to fend for themselves as orphans, the oldest of whom is a sixteen-year-old girl who is extremely vulnerable to being raped without anyone to protect her. It makes me mad. Our AIDS project, meanwhile, continues apace with huge potential, although I fear the same relationship issues remain and prayers are needed, as the project's smooth running is key for the health of SU as a whole.

We desperately need humble and godly leadership in Christian groups in the country, and it is in very short supply.

There have recently been some high-profile corruption scandals within the church, as well as all the divisions, which have further tarnished its image in the eyes of the wider population. Sadly, I anticipate more difficulties from supposed *abakozi b'Imana* (men of God) when I return than from anyone else, as so many have corrupt motives in what they do. My life was threatened and I was nearly assassinated a while back for exposing a corrupt pastor.

There's so much bleak news, but the furnace of suffering in Africa constantly seems to churn out amazing people. I thought this week about an old Ugandan friend called Livingston. He had to flee his homeland because of the war. But despite his own troubles, he came to visit and encourage me one day when I was feeling low. He had walked for thirty days through hundreds of miles of jungle in the Congo and showed me the scar on his back where he'd been shot as he fled.

At one stage, wallowing in my self-pity, I told him how I was missing my family – and then wished I'd kept my mouth shut. Very gently, he shared that he hadn't seen or heard from his wife or kids in six years and didn't know if they were still alive or not. I felt profoundly humbled, ashamed, and challenged that this man was looking to my interests despite his much greater problems. The school of suffering has so much to teach us, and yet we seek to avoid it at all costs.

I'm heading back to Burundi shortly and am looking forward to it, although I have loved the opportunities to preach all over Britain this year, and studying at Allnations has been so refreshing, insightful, energizing and fun. It's a great place and it's a privilege to be with people who are sold out for Jesus, willing to count the cost and give their all. One single woman, off to China and leaving everything, was asked, "Aren't you afraid?" She answered, "I'm afraid of only one thing: that I should become a grain of wheat not willing to die."

Amen! I choose, along with Paul, to "consider everything a loss compared to the surpassing greatness of knowing Christ Jesus my Lord" (Philippians 3:8). We must live lives which are compelling in their authenticity. Yet, the following words by Os Guinness are the most convicting I've read over the last few months:

> Put differently, in the decades I have followed Jesus, second only to the joy of knowing Him has been a sorrow at the condition of those of us today who name ourselves His followers. If so many of us profess to live by the Gospel, yet are so pathetically marginal to the life of our societies and so nondescript and inconsequential in our individual lives, is there something wrong with the Gospel, or does the problem lie with us?

Great-aunt Rosemary and her generation are moving on to better things. *Our time is now!* So I choose to get out there, wherever He wants, in whatever capacity, and choose to be among those who "give up the best we have got to Him, our right to ourselves."

Grounds for complaint
30 August 2002

This morning, as is customary, a member of the team opened in prayer with, "Lord Jesus, thank you that we woke up this morning, that you protected us through the night and have brought us to the beginning of a new day..." These could just be ritualistic words, except that when shells are landing around the capital, you really do mean it. I have only been back a week, but on two nights there was massive shelling. The closest shell landed a mile from me, but much nearer to some of my colleagues. In fact, ten bullets went through the Bishop's house. It keeps you on your toes – well, it should at least, but I had my earplugs in and slept through it all whilst the others in the house were gathered in one room together, wondering whether they should wake me up!

I thank God that all our team members have been protected and the office was undamaged, although it was near the main military installation being targeted at the time. Not such good news greeted me on my arrival, as my flat-mate was up-country assessing the damage of the latest rebel incursion. She had refused to pay a "contribution" to the rebel cause and this was perhaps the result. At the time I was boarding the plane in England, the rebels were pillaging the health center, setting the ambulance on fire, and nearly killing Claver, her main colleague there. He was shot at four times and hit twice, but they were only minor injuries, and he was back wanting to work the next day! Some people out here are simply amazing.

There is still the usual mixture of encouragements and discouragements. As I drove to preach at a new church on Sunday morning, having been at the lakeside at 7.00 a.m. to see several hundred people baptized, I was full of joy, because the body of Christ is growing fast. But then this old lady hobbled across the road in front of me. Her sunken eyes were utterly lifeless. I tooted for her to get out of the way and she stopped in her tracks, expressionless. I had to swerve, as she didn't bother moving. I felt like crying – she looked like the living dead – a picture of complete despair.

As I listen to the shooting and shelling, and see the desperate poverty, I am gutted that fifteen months after my departure, things haven't got any better. In fact, they may even be worse, and the Burundian franc was devalued by 20 per cent this week, which will further cripple the vast majority who are desperately eking out an existence. Picture the family where they share one pair of shoes, so whoever goes into town wears them that day, whilst the others stay at home. I bought an evangelist friend of mine a pair of shoes. He sheepishly asked me to give him $10, explaining that every time he preached he borrowed a pair from somebody different, but everyone was getting fed up with him, and it was all so shameful for a "man of God". Meanwhile, senior Christian leaders are bitterly taking swipes at each other on the television, which is a tragic witness. Unity remains elusive. Hopefully at SU we can play a role in helping to restore it.

I came back here last week in order to be in time for SU's Jubilee celebration – twenty-five years in action in Burundi. We had a big party and it was a joy to see how the Lord has used the organization over the years and kept it going through some difficult times. It was the main article on the televised news in the evening, so we got lots of positive coverage and publicity.

On a personal level, I'm thrilled to be back on the front line in Burundi. My time at Allnations was very beneficial in sharpening my vision and philosophy, and I have returned with a much more thought-through and strategic approach. For my first three years in Burundi, I traveled around the country at breakneck speed, preaching and teaching anywhere and everywhere, and it was totally unsustainable, albeit extremely fruitful. It will be much more effective now to begin to identify the best local leaders who combine gifting, vision, integrity and passion, and get behind them to empower and equip a new generation to transform the nation. So that's my plan and I trust the Lord to guide me in it.

In any case, it's good to be home. I have a deep peace about being safely at the heart of God's dangerous will for my life. The big downer is that I have an allergy to something in Burundi which kicks in almost as soon as I arrive. It's very debilitating and makes it easy for me to sink into despair. But how can I complain? The other day, I asked a colleague who lives in a shack containing open sewage how he managed to smile so much, bearing in mind his personal circumstances. He didn't mean it that way, but his answer served as a rebuke to me: "Simon, how can I complain when I have my Jesus?"

How do you answer that?

A friend's assassination
8 September 2002

Last night was Rick's leaving do at the US Security Chief's house, the place I stayed when I was getting death threats a while back. We heard a few rounds being shot, but it didn't last. I met a lady who turned out to be from the royal family and I quizzed her about her view on politics and the current situation. I asked her what she did at weekends. She replied that she went to weddings and funerals, mostly funerals, which were happening all the time.

And then early this morning my colleague DD rang me up. That seemingly innocuous round of bullets last night? It was a contract killing of dear Thierry, a wonderful brother who has been doing some high-level behind-the-scenes strategic initiatives to broker peace.

Devastating.

There are lots of theories emerging as to who is responsible, but nobody really knows, and it'll probably go unsolved. We went round to see his precious wife, Imelda, and their kids, who were in shock and obviously hadn't really taken in what was going on. She seemed serene but the truth no doubt hasn't sunk in. This is a real blow.

Last night…

26 September 2002

One of my current flatmates, Andrea, has just sent this to me from the hellish reality of her Tearfund emergency feeding facility down South in Makamba:

What did you do last night?

I watched a child die… a boy called Pierre. A little boy, four years old – a child who should have just been starting to discover the joys of the world.

We found him yesterday at the displaced camp where he lived near the Tanzanian border. His auntie brought him along to our nutritional screening. His condition was critical, he had severe anemia, so we transferred him to our Therapeutic Feeding Center along with fourteen others yesterday. He and the rest of his family came together – they were all malnourished. In the car my colleague Jane thought she was going to lose him, but he made it to the center. The six of them took up three beds – that's three quarters of the section reserved for the most serious cases.

During the night Pierre slipped into a coma but came round again. We gave him a blood transfusion through a vein in the side of his head.

We drove to the feeding station at 1.30 a.m. Pierre was in the first bed on the right. His gaunt little face with large, blank, staring eyes was a picture of pain and despair. His auntie didn't seem to have any emotions. She lay bare-chested with a baby attempting to feed at each shriveled, empty breast. I was wearing a fleece and still felt cold. Pierre was propped up against her with his feet dangling over the side of the bed, sighing with every breath. The other tiny little one carried on breast-feeding, oblivious to his cousin's pain. He didn't understand what was happening. Meantime Pierre was growing weaker and weaker.

He looked like a skin-clad skeleton.

We all prayed silently in our hearts. It's so hard to know what to pray. "Come on, make it, hang in there!" But do we really want this child to come through and carry on suffering in such pitiful conditions? Surely he has a right to live? He's four – he has hardly even lived yet. But at the same time, surely he'd be better off lying peacefully in the loving arms of the Father, pain over, and leaving his war-torn land behind him.

Every time he stopped sighing we held our breath. It was feeding time and all the other babies were crying, but silence here. Then he sighed again and we too breathed a sigh of relief.

We gave him hydrocortisone by IV to perk him up. We gave him a diuretic. He was on antibiotics. We had done everything and there was nothing more to do, so we waited and paced up and down. Either we would pace until morning and there would be no change or he would die.

At 3.30 a.m. Pierre took his last few shallow breaths and his blank eyes continued to stare, but this time no more desperate sighs. His auntie closed his eyes and started to sob. We covered his little body with a blanket. Silently Jane put her arm around the woman, a terrible sense of loss.

A few other mothers gathered round and prayed. We drove home in silence at 3.45 a.m.

What can I say?

No words will do. I just bow my head and weep.

Into the bush
11 October 2002

What a day! First of all, I slept terribly, having woken up bitten raw by three mosquitoes trapped inside my net. Then I went to pick up a number of people to go up north to Muyinga for a weekend of outreach, but of course they weren't ready. Eventually we got under way and prayed for our journey. There was no sign of trouble on the roads. Everything went well for the first two hours as far as Kayanza, where we picked up another pastor, but then as we approached Ngozi, I had to pull over because something was clearly wrong. Only because of what happened earlier this week (the bolts on a wheel were stolen and we had to go and buy them back off the friendly thieves in Buyenzi!) did I check the wheels and, lo and behold, the rear left one was about to fall off, a few of the bolts having come loose. We shifted the bolts from another wheel, made it to Ngozi, and had lunch whilst we commissioned someone to find us some more. But bolts are like gold-dust here and he couldn't get any. We decided to risk it and left, but within a few miles we had the same problem. We had to jack up the car four times altogether and lost another bolt, so we were down to the bare minimum. We were thinking of phoning Bujumbura to send out another truck, but that would mean a four-hour wait. Finally, we tried the dodgy-looking spare tire, whose bolts had less damage to them, and in the end we chanced it all the way to Muyinga, claiming a safe journey and rejoicing in advance that great things would happen, as the enemy was trying so hard to stop us getting there.

We headed another 50 km beyond the town of Muyinga, along the Tanzanian border, into the middle of nowhere. One thing that really struck me was the explosive growth of Islam. It is Friday, so that is their special time anyway, but they are increasing in numbers so fast, even in these far outposts. The largely nominal State Catholicism in Burundi seems to have precious little to offer of any substance, so it is almost as though it is a free-for-all between Islam and Protestants. We drove past one mosque which was not there two years ago when I last came through these parts. Islam is visibly spreading whilst the Christians are too busy engaged in petty squabbles and infighting. Come on, church leaders, wake up!

We were mobbed on our arrival by a frenzied crowd of people who were so happy to see us. They had been praying, as there had been a phone call saying that we had broken down. Some of them would never have seen a white man before, so lots just wanted to touch me. The meeting had recently finished, as we were so late, but they reconvened just so that we could greet the assembly, and we promptly decided to show a film, after which DD preached, whilst Pio and I went off to sort out accommodation with the local Catholics. The head Father was a Ugandan missionary, whose pidgin Kirundi is very different to mine, but equally bad. We picked the others up and there was a massive response as DD preached to them.

The two of us shared a dingy room. There is no electricity or water, we really are isolated. So here I am by candlelight, with a mattress on the floor, in one of the most remote places in Africa. Wow! This life is so amazing, fulfilling, varied and challenging. I praise God for the privilege of being here.

Kick-starting the church
12 October 2002

Word got around and many people came to our meetings. People literally walked for several hours to come. Although we were blatantly the new kids in town, we were greeted everywhere by beaming smiles, waves and shouts of "Praise the Lord!" These people are so very poor and needy. A lot of them really smell, I guess because of their old clothes and not getting the chance to wash often – the nearest source of water being many miles away. They really need rain and yet there seems to be so much joy as well. People eagerly grabbed our hands to greet us whenever we stopped to get out of the jeep.

I preached in the afternoon to a packed church with a

raucous atmosphere. It was a wonderful time and the meeting was very short, as we had got permission to show the *Jesus* film on the main football field, which was 4 km away, and people needed time to walk there. Many came – I am guessing at 3,000 – and, as ever, it was fantastic, with hundreds responding to my colleague Juvenal's preach. The potential of a weekend like this is to completely kick-start a new dimension of growth in the local church. The local pastors are on fire, so there should be good follow-up. May the fruit be lasting! I came back tired and elated.

Hungry for the gospel
13 October 2002

I came down with dysentery during the night and therefore hardly slept at all. Pio caught me repeatedly yawning in the church service. They had built a makeshift stage outside the church in anticipation of the extra numbers, and it was needed because lots more people came, walking for miles to get there. About twenty kids sheltered from the sun under the stage itself and I feared that it might collapse and kill them, since the supports were just odd stumps and branches, hardly the sturdiest of constructions. Thankfully, although the sun was out, there were clouds too, which was a relief for the crowds of people.

When we left in the morning, our Catholic friends gave us a bargain rate for our use of their accommodation, "in the name of ecumenism", which we were very grateful for. They were lovely people, clearly very lonely, and not interested in gospel chats at all. But friendships were formed and addresses exchanged, so who knows if they will look us up when they come to the capital. We had lunch at a pastor's house and there discovered quite how far they had to walk to get water. Had I known, I would not have been so wasteful in my use of it.

We left and as we drove along the road, there were streams of people for miles who were slowly heading home. My confidence was growing that the wheels would last, but I was aware that we would be in serious trouble if a tire burst. We got to the main road and then to Muyinga where we picked up DD, who said that he struggled to find a single believer in the whole town. There is a lot of work for us to do in this area of the country. DD had again tried to go to the site where his father was murdered in 1993, but was warned away as he approached. His actions may have been construed as inflammatory and provocative. There was no diesel at any of the petrol stations in the town, so we left and hoped we had enough in the tank to make it the 85 km to Ngozi. Thankfully, we made it, filled up, and continued beyond to Kayanza, to spend the night at a Catholic sisters' retreat center.

The retreat center was both beautiful and calm, but I called a friend in the capital and discovered that, unlike the peace here, there had been a lot of shooting in the Kanyosha suburb the previous night. This is Juvenal's part of town, but he spoke to his family and they were all safe. We went to the local inn for supper and sat there discussing our dreams for this country. There are so many needs crying out to be met, so many valid areas of ministry are being neglected, and the potential is simply huge. I must not take the whole burden on myself – it is the Lord's – but I can't help feeling at one and the same time a mixture of both excitement and heaviness at the burden of responsibility. But what a wonderful weekend – it's a massive privilege to be called to this kind of work. We're trusting we make it safely back to Bujumbura early tomorrow morning, once the roads have been opened. Praise the Lord!

How hungry?

5 December 2002

Someone once asked me: "How much do you want of God?"

What would you answer?

Their answer was: "Because nobody has less of God than they want."

Do you think that's right? It could also have something to do with how much I let God have of me. An example: Last week I was with Tearfund in Makamba, in the far South. The team had just completed a corporate three-day fast to plead with the Lord for the release of their colleague and friend Adelbert's sister, who was kidnapped two months ago by Mai Mai rebels from the neighboring Congo. He was near giving up and presumed she was dead. But when we drove back to Bujumbura together, he phoned up straight away and heard that she had been released on the last day of the fast! We were all blown away and one of the team said, "When we've got so much power available in prayer and fasting, why don't we use it more?"

It made me think that maybe it's because we simply don't want that much of God. How hungry am I to see Him work in my life? What price am I willing to pay? Do I really believe what I profess regarding His absolute right to my life? Or do I simply pay lip service to the lyrics of the worship songs I lustily sing in church on Sunday?

It has been an emotional few days. My Kenyan flatmate Anne's son, Daniel, went missing in Nairobi. He had left home as usual to go to school and seven days later he was still nowhere to be found. There was naturally a real heaviness in the house. It was horrible. Lots of prayers were offered up. And then the dreaded call came. Her uncle relayed the news: "Are you ready? He's alive!" He had been taken at gunpoint, driven into the bush, stripped, tied up but then abandoned.

The motive for the attack remains unclear. A herd-boy then wandered by with his goats, spotted him and freed him. Daniel stumbled 200 km through the forest, before his exhausted and tick-ridden body was discovered collapsed outside somebody's house. But he was alive and we were laughing and hugging and singing with joy.

What I considered my most important week of the year, doing another Evangelism Explosion (EE) training session, was a huge success. We were equipping pastors and laypeople to go out and share their faith, as well as to be able to train others to do likewise. The enemy fought it hard, with materials going astray on the regional director's flight here, the Satanist next door causing us trouble, one trainer never arriving after having a motorbike crash, another having to miss most of the week as a family member had died, and the rebels launching their attack on Bujumbura during the morning of our last day. It was surreal to look up from my teaching and see plumes of smoke rise up in the hills above me as shells landed indiscriminately. So the program lived up to its name yet again – the results were indeed explosive! We went out each afternoon, working alongside a local church, going door-to-door in teams. We spoke to eighty-two people in the week, of whom forty wanted to surrender their lives to Christ. I was so thrilled to see my apprentices observe how it really worked and gain confidence to go and launch it in their respective churches.

One encouraging time I used the EE approach to share my faith when I went to the bank to deposit some money. I was talking to two lady cashiers and they asked me how it was I spoke Kirundi. I told them I was a preacher. Simultaneously they said, "Right, preach to us!"

"What? Now? Here?" I asked.

They both said an emphatic, "Yes!" So I shared the gospel for a quarter of an hour, during which nobody disturbed us.

I led them to the assurance of salvation, took their names, invited them to church with me, and we parted as friends. They were thrilled to receive our SU Bible-reading notes on my next visit and one of them invited me to meet her family.

Burundi is making the headlines more now than it has for a long time in the West. Government and rebel groups have agreed a ceasefire, but things are critically tense. It could flare up at any moment, as extremists on either side do not want to make any compromises. This week Oxfam released a briefing which sounds quite alarmist, but must be taken seriously. The poverty and suffering in the country is unimaginable. Over a million Burundians are in urgent need of food aid. I was at a therapeutic distribution center last week and saw a few of them – they were wretched, smelly, desperate and many were literally dying.

Below is a poignant excerpt from yesterday's *Independent* newspaper in the UK:

> On a recent morning the Ndayishimiye family huddled from the seasonal rains in their tin-roof hut. The women wept softly, the men were stony-faced. An army soldier had just murdered their daughter Jeanine, a Tutsi. "He demanded to see her ID card," said Renovat, a cousin standing by a puddle stained with her blood. "She handed him the Bible and said that was her identity. He got angry and started shooting."

Very sad – but a powerful witness to what our message is as followers of Jesus. And as always, when so many are being killed around us, we are confronted with the necessity of being ready to meet our Maker. A friend of mine in hospital was woken up the other night by incessant knocking at 3 a.m. A woman needed his help to lift her husband to the toilet. He begrudgingly crawled out of bed and lugged the man to and from the lavatory. But before going back to bed, he asked the man if he could return in the morning to tell him about Jesus. The man replied, "No, if you want to tell me about Jesus, tell me right now, because I might be dead by the morning." My friend spoke of the love and mercy of God and the lady watched her husband pray to receive Christ. In the morning he was indeed dead. But at least he was ready.

9

PEACE ON A KNIFE-EDGE

STOP PRESS: Explosive developments in Burundi!
1 January 2003

Happy New Year to you all!

Amazingly, peace is still holding out, which I am thrilled about and astonished by, I must admit. Keep praying. As ever, these are critical times. I shed a tear yesterday at the thought that, yes, we may actually find a lasting peaceful solution for this land. It is hard to conceive as we enter the tenth year of civil war. Please, Lord!

The start of this year has brought some fairly seismic developments for me. I have had a miserable time with my health recently with amoebic dysentery, flu and malaria over the festive period. As I write this, I am still weak and feeble with malaria. But my best friend came out to see me and we had a great street kids' party on the beach, as well as a youth camp up-country and a trip to Rwanda!

That was when I was knocked out with malaria. But on New Year's Day, I gingerly crawled out of bed and the two of us borrowed a friend's motorboat for a trip on Lake Kivu. We headed out into the distance, surrounded by an eerie quiet in the early morning haze. After a while, far out in the deep, we came across a random red balloon floating on the surface with an envelope attached in a plastic bag. My friend fished it out of the water, opened up the envelope, and tried reading the message, only understanding the last line of the scrawl in English, which read: "Lizzie Corfe, will you marry me?" I then got down on one knee, proposed to her, we hugged, and then prayed a prayer of radical surrender to the Lord for the rest of our lives together. Afterwards I went back to bed feeling rough and sorry for myself!

So who is this Lizzie? She's a primary school teacher who has recently spent two years in Nepal. She's incredibly feisty and fun, able to challenge me and keep me in check, far holier than me, ready for a crazy life, and just sheer quality! We're planning to get married this coming summer.

AIDS – not a starfish statistic
24 January 2003

A little boy was running along the beach in the aftermath of a big storm. Thousands upon thousands of starfish had been washed up by the waves and were lying scattered across the sand. In his youthful zeal, the boy picked up starfish upon starfish and threw them energetically back into the water. As he did so, a cynical old man strolled past, and said to him:

"Hey, what are you doing?"

"I'm saving all these starfish, because if they don't get back into the water, they'll die."

"But just take a look: there are tens of thousands of starfish as far as you can see. You're wasting your time. What's the point? What difference will it make?"

The boy listened thoughtfully, then bent over, scooped another starfish up and launched it back into the sea. Then he turned to look the man in the eye, and declared:

"Well, it made a difference to that one!"

What difference can we make? Where shall we start? What is the point, considering all we are up against? I am currently in South Africa on a preaching tour and for three days my life has been consumed with Bongani. You probably know the films, *Three Men and a Baby/Little Lady*. For us, it was *Three Men and Little Bongani*. Meet the team:

- **Anthony Farr.** South African, 30 years old, ex-merchant banker. He left his lucrative career because he is a "dreamer of the day", a visionary and a risk-taker who wanted to move beyond success to significance. He co-founded Starfish with the aim of turning the tide on AIDS in South Africa.

- **Peter Barnett.** Australian, 31 years old. Peter is a Rhodes scholar, solicitor, an exceptional man and general good egg.

- **Simon Guillebaud.** English, 29 years old. I'm just someone who said yes to God's call and opted for the adventure of living instead of the safety of existing.

- **Bongani.** South African, 9 years old. A little boy who is dying of AIDS.

The clinic thought Bongani would die last month. But he is scared of dying and is a stubborn little fellow, so he ate despite himself, regained some strength and proved them wrong. His fears of death are understandable, having been left traumatized after watching his mum and dad die of AIDS within the space of a few months. He was then taken in by his grandmother. As often happens, his friend's mother recently died. Bongani explained to his friend, "Now they are going to take your mum and put her in a dark hole, cover her with rocks and soil, and she will stay there forever all by herself." The little friend cried and said he wouldn't let them do that to his mum. But Bongani replied, "You can't cry, because that's just the way it is."

Bongani's dream, before he would die, was to go to the coast, play in the sand and swim in the sea. So we took him to Durban, a six-hour drive from Johannesburg. During the journey he was quiet and withdrawn and he looked so skinny and sad. Initially his eyes were lifeless and he was no doubt confused about these three weirdoes who were making ridiculous noises all the time, trying to make him laugh. But slowly and surely he relaxed and loosened up. He stuffed his face with food when we ate at the service station and chuckled huskily on the trampoline in the kiddies' play area. Eventually we made it to the beach and then his eyes lit up. We got ready in the car park and tentatively ventured onto the sand. The waves were huge, so we held him tightly as we paddled into the sea. One crashing wave scared him and he'd soon had enough. He fell silent again, but his dream had come true.

We spent another two days at "God's Golden Acre", a center where dozens of underprivileged or orphaned kids had been taken in. Bongani never talked, just nodding with his head if we asked him a question. But in the afternoon I took him to the shallow pool. He gripped me around the neck. Slowly I drew away and he jumped into my arms. Growing in confidence, he began splashing further from me and then feigned drowning, saying, "I'm sinking!" That was the first sign of his humor and his unquenchable little spirit. He was so precious.

On the long drive back to Johannesburg, I lay in the rear of the truck on a mattress and tried to sleep. Bongani snuggled up sideways to me and nestled his forehead on my temple as I lay on my back looking at the roof. He slept and his sporadic sighs occasionally interrupted the more constant snoring emanating from his snotty nostrils. It grew colder as dusk set in and he clung tight. It broke my heart that my new little friend would soon be dead. Anthony had flummoxed me with the question, "What is God's purpose for Bongani's life?" Can you help me with the answer? One thing I do know is that I'll never forget him.

We dropped him off at school where his buxom granny worked as a cleaner. She had already buried three of her daughters who had died of AIDS. Bongani hesitated to leave my side, but I pushed him towards her. His sheepish eyes and timid grin were the last I saw of him as we walked back silently to the car, tears flowing on the inside, if not the outside.

What was the point?

What difference did that trip make?

Within the next seven years, according to projections, there will be 2 million AIDS orphans in South Africa. Faced with such facts, we can give up and bury our heads in the sand, or we can get involved – and that applies to whatever challenge God lays before us. One by one, bit by bit, we'll get there. His call and challenge to me are in Burundi. For Anthony, it is in South Africa. How about you? What is He saying to you now? Are you listening? Are you responding?

The morality of war

1 March 2003

I thought I'd write down my feelings before the war begins in Iraq and little, insignificant, oilless Burundi is even more forgotten than usual. I don't want to open a can of worms, but

I feel so deeply angry at the world's injustices and outraged at the moral high ground that my own country and the USA are claiming right now. This morning as I write I'm listening to the sounds of shelling and machine guns as people are being murdered a few miles away – *right now!* Who kindly makes the weapons for these misguided Burundians to blow each other's limbs off? The USA and UK.

Of course, we all want to get rid of Saddam, but please, Bush and Blair, let's be honest and not claim we're doing it on the basis of "morality". When did morality ever come into foreign policy? It's money that makes your (and many of our) worlds go round.

Having just been ridiculously reductionist and simplistic (yes, I do realize it), let's have a look at what war does. How about an authentic example from Ruyigi this week, where fighting has been raging between the army and the country's largest rebel group?

Maison Shalom, a Catholic medical clinic far up in the hills of Ruyigi, has been completely overrun and overwhelmed by the arrival of thirteen malnourished babies with bulging stomachs and oversized heads. They lie two by two in cribs in five different rooms. Most of their mothers died during childbirth; others were killed while fleeing the fighting, leaving their babies helpless in the bush. Some babies were brought to the shelter after three weeks in the bush, only to die on arrival. Of a total of eighteen such babies brought in last week, five have since died. The others are undergoing intense medical care. "Eighteen newborn babies mean that eighteen mothers have died helplessly. Things have gone too far. Silence is complicity," said the main lady there, Marguerite Barankitse. Meanwhile, these dirt-poor, unfortunate people whose babies die are charged $10 to get the body back to give "it" a decent burial, but many can't afford that sum, so the callous authorities just throw away the bundle of flesh. This is not war and its consequences, in the abstract. It is the stark reality and far removed from the pristine corridors of political power or our comfy suburban living rooms.

Boom! Boom! Another two shells. In the next few days I may find out that one of those big bangs killed someone I care about, as happened a few months ago. Last weekend my team drove up to Kayanza in the North, which had been attacked twice in the week, with pitched battles in the town at night. It was quiet for our visit and we were able to show a film to a massive crowd as well as preach and worship together. One group of people arrived at 4 p.m., having set off on foot forty miles away at 4 a.m. I was profoundly humbled by such a demonstration of spiritual hunger. How far would I walk to listen to someone talking about Jesus? Many were touched by the Lord.

We were due to go up-country this weekend as well, but have put it off for a couple of weeks. Right across Burundi, there are a lot of bad things happening. In fact, these next few months will be interesting, as the Tutsi President prepares to hand over power for the second eighteen-month phase of transitional rule to a Hutu. It is extremely tense and people are very pessimistic about the peace process.

I continue in daily prayer for peace – in Iraq, as well as in Burundi. And also for (another shell just landed) the leaders and shapers of our global village (and again) to have wisdom and integrity of motive in what they decide, which may not directly affect their gross affluence, but certainly does affect untold millions of faceless and voiceless souls who wallow in misery and oppression.

We shouldn't need a war in Iraq to get us on our knees. We're all to be engaged in spiritual warfare and the battle is just as real in the West, although maybe more subtle. Should I apologize for the angry tone of this rant? Well, it's from my heart and it's how I feel. Many won't agree with me, but I suspect that's because they only see it from the comfort and safety of their armchairs.

Explosive results
25 March 2003

I cannot think of anything in life that I would rather be doing than going into the hills and sharing the good news of Jesus Christ with those who haven't yet heard about Him, and teaching and empowering others to do the same. Two of us went to Matana a couple of weeks ago to train several dozen Bible students in Evangelism Explosion. Now we are back for the exams and actual visiting. Enough theory, now it's time to put it into practice! And what a day! I slept atrociously in my tent, with my gut on fire from all the beans they are feeding us, and the night-watchmen talking ridiculously loudly from 4 a.m., so I got up at the crack of dawn to pray and prepare. I bought some horrible biscuits, which had a hint of paraffin in them, but I was assured that was on purpose to prevent constipation – as every good scout knows! I had a real sense of anticipation (no, not constipation!) for the day ahead. The potential is so huge and we have put so much work into this. How would it go?

After the morning meditation the exams took place. It soon dawned on me that most of the students were going to fail. The Institute guys are doing a degree and so are perfectly competent – that is eleven of them – but the rest, about twenty-five, are at the Bible school, and some did not get beyond primary education level as children. We had packed a thirteen-week course into just four intensive days and it was just too much for them. The oral exams were abysmal, so by lunchtime Elihud (my co-trainer) and I were discouraged and thinking it was going to be a complete failure. We had a team meeting and agreed to reconvene after lunch, when we would go out visiting and at least show them how it was done...

... and *hallelujah!* The afternoon was quite extraordinary. The fact that we are up-country means that I am a novelty sight as a white man, so I can't fail to draw a crowd. That is a mixed blessing when we are trying to show others how to lead individuals or small groups to faith. But off we drove in the minibus, dropping other groups at different locations along the way. There were nine groups in all. I had five apprentices with me. We stopped on the road outside two huts which turned out to be grimy drinking dens. Within a couple of minutes of pulling up, there were forty drunks gathered around on benches and chairs to listen to us. I preached, having to talk fast and loudly to try to keep their attention, mixing French and Kirundi. Claude, my apprentice and an Anglican minister, translated where needed. Some laughed, some were distracted, some slobbered, and some listened attentively. Just about all of them were willing to join in the prayer at the end and they packed us off with some hearty back-slapping and banter.

Another few miles down the road we saw two young lads collecting water at a pump. I thought that would be better – a smaller group and therefore more chance to keep their attention – but within minutes sixty school children had appeared out of nowhere. The kids gathered around us and wouldn't go away, so I preached again. When I said that we were leaving they all bellowed in unison that we couldn't leave but must carry on preaching. The same thing happened again, twice, before we eventually headed off after praying for them all.

Then we stopped off in the middle of nowhere by an old man tending his cows. He must have been frightened to see six men jump out of a van and walk purposefully towards him! He was quite evasive, and I don't blame him, so a few of us withdrew. Then Claude accosted two young lads on their bike, and he led them superbly to the Lord after nearly an hour. It was so encouraging to watch. Meanwhile, the others were witnessing to the old man, who opened up a bit more as they took over the tending of his cows! The young lads prayed with Claude, who was buzzing afterwards, and I was buzzing that Claude was buzzing because empowering people to do this stuff is just so exciting! The lads said they would cycle to church on Sunday.

We drove back towards Matana and picked up another group on the way who had also had a great time. We were all singing away in the minibus as I drove them home and when we parked by the church they carried on singing jubilantly, so we did three more laps before coming to a standstill, laughing and praising God. The feedback session was hugely positive. One student said to me, "Simon, you will have to find us more bricks to build a bigger church, as the cathedral won't be big enough at this rate!" *Hallelujah!* The lights had come on in nearly all of the trainees and we were all praising the Lord. The closing prayer was thunderous and we headed off for a quality night's rest.

Innocent casualties
28 March 2003

8.27 p.m., Friday night – the President has just announced on the radio that he will definitely hand over to the Vice-President on 1 May, and there is full-on shooting and shelling going on as I type this. We have just been contacted through the embassy representative and told not to leave the house unless absolutely necessary.

I have an official report before me by Human Rights Watch about what happened in Burundi last month – stories of arbitrary rapes and murders by soldiers and rebels alike. Seven believers were holding an all-night prayer meeting in Ruyigi province when soldiers came to the house, took them away, and executed them all. I have just got back safely from the South, but when we left Bujumbura to go there on Monday a colleague warned me that in her part of town they were talking of an imminent rebel attack, so I wasn't sure if we would be stranded up-country amidst full-scale war. As it turns out, it was yet another false alarm, and hopefully what is going on right now will peter out too, but it illustrates the tension and fragility of the peace process. Few people expect there to be a peaceful transition, and with just over a month to go to the key handover date, let's pray Burundi is not as morbidly dramatic a place to observe on television as the 24/7 coverage of what is going on in Iraq – not that there will be any cameras or significant interest in what is going on out here...

10

A CHRISTIANITY THAT RUINS YOUR LIFE

What happened to radical Christianity, the un-nice brand of Christianity that turned the world upside down?... I'm ready for a Christianity that "ruins" my life, that captures my heart and makes me uncomfortable.

Robert Capon

Tears for Burundi
26 April 2003

We've just had a very emotional time. SU have been running a youth camp for three hundred pupils over four days. As is often the case, there's no running water at all, so it has been quite a smelly affair! However, these guys are seriously passionate and it has been a wonderful time of worshipping, sharing and teaching. During my farewell preach I said I was returning to England to get married, I'd be gone for a while, and for some, we may never see each other again on this earth. My voice faltered and a number of us were crying. We are all full of faith, ready for anything that might come our way, looking forward to heaven, and rejoicing in that security despite the desperate state of the nation. Still, it broke my heart to think of what might happen to some of them before Lizzie and I return next year. A dear Burundian friend pleaded with me: "Please don't stop crying for Burundi, there are so many Burundians who can no longer cry for themselves."

"Safety is not in the absence of danger, but in the presence of God!"
2 May 2003

I've been back in the UK for a couple of days and I got out just before things heated up somewhat. Below is an email from my flatmate out there:

> Now it really is happening in Burundi and you are not here to inform the international media of our plight! I got back from Bukavu last Saturday when it really got nasty. Mortars started landing on Thursday and things got progressively worse. On Saturday night around 10.30 p.m. the most almighty noise zoomed over our heads. Everyone literally dived for cover. We sheltered in the corridor for two hours. It was a mixture of exhilaration and terror as we counted the seconds between launch and landing, closing our eyes while we waited for the impact. A couple of mortars landed 200 meters from the house. We were called to an emergency meeting on Sunday and by Tuesday we had evacuated with reports that the rebels had stolen mortars from the army and would use them.

Another friend wrote:

> I can't believe you left us in this war zone! You had a lucky escape. The rebels started bombing or shelling Bujumbura last

Thursday at 6.00 a.m. It went on all day until the evening and they began getting closer. You could hear the rockets whistling through the air and then landing. However, we weren't really scared as we thought they would never come to Kinindo and we carried on as normal. We all went to the pool and had a lovely time with the shelling going on as background noise! Then Saturday night it started at the same time and you could hear them whistling over the house and crashing as they landed. People kept calling us and saying, "Get outside!" Then someone else would call and say, "Get inside and hide in the corridor!" Apparently the rebels were launching rockets from the lake. Our gatekeeper Manuel was trying to tell us that all was fine and kept saying, "No problem!" and then one landed very near and he jumped in the flowerbed! On Sunday everyone was panicking and we have heard all sorts of rumors. The Tearfunders have evacuated to Nairobi. However, since Saturday night all has been quiet despite anticipated attacks. I went to the American Embassy on Monday night and they said they thought the shelling would continue, but they reassured us that the rebels didn't have very powerful rockets.

I had very mixed emotions as I read the above, wanting to be with my precious friends and colleagues at such a time. But, here I am, back in England, getting ready to tie the knot in a few months. We have just set up a charity in the UK called Great Lakes Outreach (GLO) because I had briefly become an al Qaeda suspect, due to the fact that I was receiving so many small personal donations and then taking out massive lump sums of cash because of the dysfunctional banking system in Burundi! Apparently, I was the stereotypical profile of an al Qaeda mule, so the British Government was ringing up and asking who on earth I was, and could I kindly set up something more obviously financially transparent and accountable!

"Nothing will stop us…"
9 July 2003

Just a month before our wedding things were looking very grim again, so I sent out this urgent request for prayer:

This is an SOS plea for urgent prayer as another attack is unleashed on the capital. The rebels infiltrated from the South at the beginning of the week and that is where our offices are. Two days ago my source at the UN said twenty-seven are dead, but various people are updating me through each day, and both the death toll and numbers of people fleeing are rising. I have had no news from my precious colleagues and I long to know they are alive and well.

You will appreciate how heavily this is weighing on me and the feeling is exacerbated by the fact that I am currently in the USA (Charleston, South Carolina) doing a lot of preaching and sharing about Burundi. Charleston is one of the safest, nicest, friendliest and wealthiest places on the planet, in sharp contrast to Burundi, and I am trying, amongst other things, to sensitize people here to make them aware of how horrific things are elsewhere in this sick world beyond their own back yard. I have experienced nothing but fantastic hospitality and generosity, but I can't help feeling internally shredded and confused by the gross disparities between these nations in terms of justice and wealth distribution, and by the thoughts of my imperiled loved ones in Burundi sheltering from the shelling. Other grim events are going on there *right now* as I write and you read this. In my last meeting I just burst into tears, which took everyone by surprise, including me, although the wonderful group of people handled this blubbering Brit with amazing aplomb!

I am not in Burundi to report first hand at present, but the flatmates I left a couple of months ago still are. One writes:

7th July: I am sat under my mosquito net listening to the noise outside. I woke up at 4 a.m. to the familiar sound of machine gun fire. Shots and mortar rounds ring out in the night sky. They are dropping some heavy rounds and I don't think sleep is an option. Apparently it's in Kanyosha which is 2 km from here. Most of the team are now awake. It's not a nice welcome for the two new arrivals. It's strange how things kick off here. Just yesterday we were playing volleyball on the beach and it could have been on any beach in the Mediterranean. Then twelve hours later, "Boom!" Why can't they stop this crazy fighting? We will probably find out tomorrow that no one's been hurt apart from a few cows! In fact, the birds are starting their dawn chorus, totally oblivious to the human vagaries of fighting.

I finally put my earplugs in and was woken up by Anne shaking my arm at 9 a.m.! I somehow slept through the bombs and my alarm clock. It is still continuing and no one is going anywhere at the moment. I've heard fighting before, but it's been quiet since the elections. We have just had a prayer meeting amidst the backdrop of shells. Our house is in a safe part of town and unlike most of the population, we could get out if things got really bad.

12:00hrs: We've been called to work. The UN announced it was safe to go to work, but I can still hear the thud of mortar fire. I am staying put.

15:00hrs: Quick sortie to collect emergency rations. Traffic in town is reduced but people are still going about their daily business. Managed to get fresh fruit and veg, rice and beans (standard going-to-ground fare).

16:40hrs: Helicopters are flying overhead. Up until now it was thought the military only had one helicopter, but now there are three circling the city. I have never seen bombs being dropped from a plane, but now I can see a large object falling from the helicopter. Count to five... an almighty bang... then smoke rising.

The helicopters return for another attack – this time grey tracers and red shots from out of the front. It sounds like crackling fireworks, then they land with multiple booms.

17:35hrs: Helicopters have reloaded and are back for another bomb drop.

18:00hrs: UN forbids all movements. Everyone is back at base awaiting the events of the evening.

I have just received another email from a Burundian friend:

Simon, things are terrible. As I write, bombs are falling across the city. I hear that your offices have been taken over and are being used by the rebels as their base. I don't think you know any of the dead… more later. Send us anything you can find for us to help in relieving those worst struck. We want to help, but we have nothing. Having said that, nothing will stop us serving our God and claiming His promises for this land – all works for good to those that love Him!

Please pray!

Incidentally, the death toll in just one part of town, Kanyosha, where our office was, was 325 people (at least those were the official figures), most of whom were 11- to 15-year-old child soldiers sent in as cannon fodder by their cowardly superiors. In a sick twist, high on drugs, they launched their attack singing worship songs. Three of GLO's partners (Harvest for Christ, Youth for Christ and New Generation) sent teams of young people into Kanyosha over the next few days to redeem those worship songs and minister to the traumatized people by cleaning away the bodies and rubble, and practically showing the love of Christ.

Radical Christianity
10 September 2003

Greetings from a newly married and honeymooned man! Yes, Lizzie and I are just back from three fabulous weeks in France after a superb wedding on 16 August. The only issue of concern on our big day came during the vows. We had learned them off by heart, but Lizzie hesitated at one point and forgot to "love, cherish *and obey*," so I'm slightly worried that there'll be insurrection in the ranks at some stage!

We're back at Allnations where I'm on the Masters program and Lizzie will do a Diploma. Everyone said we couldn't possibly spend our first year of marriage in a war zone, so I have reluctantly heeded their advice. But having done so, I am now really excited about one year of further missiological studies and real quality time with my wonderwoman!

Back to Burundi and what is happening there.

After my last fraught email and a few tense days of not knowing who or how many of my colleagues and friends had been killed, news filtered through. The rebels had indeed taken over my office to use as their base. Many of these "soldiers" and innocent civilians were killed in the street fighting. There was a lot of damage to our property which we are now repairing at significant cost. But *thank God* none of my colleagues were among the hundreds of dead, although sadly our neighbor was caught up in it and killed. My awesome colleagues crept back to the office during a lull in the fighting and rescued our computers, which was very risky but a wonderful blessing in terms of saving teaching materials and copies of the coming year's Bible-reading notes for the whole nation.

In the midst of the shelling a dear Canadian friend sent me this:

Our place was pretty noisy, but otherwise fine, and the Lord blessed us with a wonderful displaced family for company and only one power cut. Water and supplies held out with the odd shopping trip. I carried on as usual. My most important near miss was a rocket ten yards away when I went into the Dept of Immigration. I took advantage to get to the head of the queue while everyone else disappeared to watch the aftermath! War stories galore, praise from the Christians, and deep gloom from the rest.

I came across these stirring words by Robert Capon:

The Good News is no longer good news, it is okay news. Christianity is no longer life-changing, it is life-enhancing. Jesus doesn't change people into wide-eyed radicals any more; He changes them into "nice people".

If Christianity is simply about being nice, I'm not interested.

What happened to radical Christianity, the un-nice brand of Christianity that turned the world upside down? What happened to the category-smashing, life-threatening, anti-institutional Gospel that spread through the first century like wildfire and was considered dangerous by those in power? What happened to the kind of Christians whose hearts were on fire, who had no fear, who spoke the truth no matter what the consequence, who made the world uncomfortable, who were willing to follow Jesus wherever He went? What happened to the kind of Christians who were filled with passion and gratitude and who every day were unable to get over the grace of God?

I'm ready for a Christianity that "ruins" my life, that captures my heart and makes me uncomfortable. I want to be filled with an astonishment which is so captivating that I am considered wild and unpredictable and, well, dangerous. Yes, I want to be "dangerous" to a dull and boring religion. I want a faith that is considered "dangerous" by our predictable and monotonous culture.

Key leader Emmanuel Ndikumana, founder of Partners Trust International, outside the new Bible School with his wife Asèle.

The Guillebaud clan – we love our little ones so much and the three of them are enough to keep us very busy, so barring medical miracles now that'll be all for us! Taking these vulnerable little lives out to Burundi was a new challenge to us as parents.

Reaching out to the marijuana crowd after our weekly early Sunday morning outreach at the beach.

Munezero Etienne, my boss in Burundi, who heads up the rapidly expanding work at Scripture Union, which has grown from employing 8 to 76 staff workers over the last decade.

Olivia Perry-Smith (GLO National Director) and Goretti Wege (KCC Manager) have worked together superbly to make the King's Conference Centre the best in the country, generating very significant sums to sow back into God's work. Long may it continue!

Onesphore, quite simply an amazing brother, who is the visionary leader of Harvest for Christ and has such a thought-through strategic vision for the whole country and beyond.

Preaching upcountry in the heat to the masses from a makeshift stage.

Our team of evangelists who reach out to Muslims, most of whom are former Muslims themselves. Most of them have had death threats. Papa Seth, second from right on the back row, was gunned down in front of his wife and kids.

Baptisms at the lake on Easter Sunday morning, although slightly nervous as there are definitely a few crocs around!

Enjoying a special event at the beach with New Generation's street kids.

A picture of the Burundian church as this woman pours out her heart to the Lord. Freddy once wrote to me: "Please don't stop shedding tears for Burundi because we've got no tears left to cry..."

Escaping from the tension with a quick break to Lake Kivu and jumping from high trees into the water below.

National Director Freddy Tuyizere, his wife Josée, and the rest of the Youth For Christ staff.

Feeding streetkids at our annual Christmas beach party. These vulnerable boys are tomorrow's murderers and rapists unless we intervene...

Standing in the burnt-out shell of what was a fuel station at Kibimba, where on 21st October 1993 a hundred school kids were locked in by a frenzied mob and then burnt alive for being from the wrong tribe.

Precious Bongani, no longer with us, one of many orphans who deeply impacted my life. With us is Anthony Farr, the founder of Starfish.

Dedicating and laying the foundation to the first house at the Gitega orphanage, on spacious land given to Youth for Christ without any bribery in a country where land is at a premium. A few years on and there is now a bustling community, with a medical clinic, a high-quality school, and several houses where the precious kids and staff live.

Amen to that! I never realized that following Jesus could, would, should be so dangerous! But as one man wrote, who was caught in an ambush and had his mouth shot off, "God never promises us an easy time, just a safe arrival." So, whether in Burundi or the USA or the UK or wherever, that is the challenge for us. We're all in a spiritual war, whether we realize it or not. We must live alert as on a battleship, not complacent as on a cruise ship.

The peace process is juddering on and the grinding poverty is not just a killer, it's a mass-murderer. Forgotten by the world's press, but close to God's heart, Burundi (and indeed neighboring Congo – a staggering 4 million dead in the last few years in the East alone, according to the latest UN statistics) needs a lasting, viable and just resolution to the deeply complex conflict. May the body of Christ play its part in the process!

Our very lifeblood
24 November 2003

It is 11.40 p.m. and I am sitting next to my precious 25-year-old cousin, Debs (who came out to visit me in Burundi with a cameraman back in 2001), in the Intensive Care Unit in Cambridge General Hospital. Two nights ago it took paramedics half an hour to cut her out of the wreckage of her car after a crash in the rain. Following several hours of surgery (stitching lacerations and binding up her liver, dealing with a punctured lung, trying to stem the loss of blood and assessing the multiple fractures), things looked bleak when I arrived. But twenty-four hours later, she is still hanging in there and has a bit more color in her bruised, swollen, stitched-up face. She brought tears to my eyes just now as she squeezed my hand and tried doing the "thumbs up", the wonderful feisty battler that she is.

I'm writing this letter as a plea for prayer in what the doctors are saying is the key time – the next twenty-four hours – when they will open up her tummy again and perform some more major and complicated surgery. The longer she lasts, the more positive we can become. She is a strong believer and was returning from a Christian conference when the crash happened. I love her dearly and am desperate for her to survive and make a full recovery. Her parents are flying back from Singapore right now and her four sisters are scattered around the globe. Many are praying and I'd love you to join them.

A prayer letter was overdue in any case on Burundi news: there have been big developments in the last week, with the main rebel group being integrated into Parliament and receiving a number of ministerial positions. Praise God for this, as even last week there was talk and fear of another, potentially imminent, *coup d'état*. The rebels are also being integrated into the army and, if that works, there is a real chance of lasting peace, although the rebel FNL still refuse to take part in the peace talks and continue to ambush and plunder both civilians and the army.

SU is moving on well, except last week a colleague of mine died – yet another victim in this humanitarian disaster, yet another to add to the daily, rising, impersonal statistic of death. His family is gutted, but most people will soon forget. Life just goes on. Life is so cheap. But no, life is so very precious.

Back to Debs. Her critical condition has made me get things back into perspective. We so easily lose sight of what really matters. It makes me want to ring up everyone I care about and tell them that I love them while I still can. It makes me look at people bustling on the wards and along the streets and see afresh the image and imprint of their Creator upon them, whether they acknowledge Him or not.

The extraordinary care Deborah is receiving makes me

want to hug all the doctors and nurses and shout at the many ungrateful grumblers who moan their lives away at the state of the National Health Service. I want to shake the millions of people who are sacrificing everything to attain a standard of living at the expense of having a life. I want to reach out to the millions who cram their lives and schedules until they are full, whilst they remain so empty.

I want to give blood (although I can't because I've had malaria too many times) which can bring life to someone else. Debs has had literally dozens of units of blood pumped into her – three times what is in her body – because she has kept on losing so much of it. But that makes me think of the ultimate sacrifice of the One who gave His blood for me – what incredible love! And in turn I want to lay down my life in His service, be it in Burundi or wherever. So may God help us to bring the lifeblood of Jesus to those dying all around us. They are on the critical list, although they do not realize it.

It transpired that a lady who was the main speaker at the conference Debs was returning from when she crashed spoke to the duty nurse on the phone as Debs was fighting for dear life. She insisted he go into the operating theatre and claim her life for God to give her a second chance. The nurse wasn't a believer and said he couldn't. But the lady refused to let the matter go, so he did (tentatively, I guess), and that was the time when things turned a corner and the surgeons were able to halt the bleeding.

In the end, after many months of astonishing results, which confounded the doctors (including her mother claiming healing for her legs when she was told Debs would never be able to walk properly again, and the bone literally growing before their eyes), Debs was able to leave hospital and rebuild her life. A year to the day after the accident, she married Bernie, with whom she was beginning to fall in love when the crash happened, and in 2010 she directed the hit film *Africa United*. Her story has inspired many since the accident and her scars are beautiful reminders of her second chance at life.

Deb's mother, my Aunt Christine, wrote the following to me:

> When I prayed for her leg, the issue was that it was set an inch too long after three months in traction and it was too painful for her to put weight on it to walk again without a crutch. I saw red when she came back distressed with the news that she would have to have a built-up shoe on the other side, probably for life, in order to walk properly again! So Hannah, Sharon and I sat her down. I had no sooner opened my mouth to say, "Lord Jesus…" than she squealed and said, "I felt that" and the hip had just shrunk back to the same length as the other leg! Well, it was still about a quarter of an inch out, but as we watched and continued praying it evened up before our eyes. Fantastic!
>
> The other instant healing was her voice, which had been damaged by the intubation when they were saving her life at the crash scene. She couldn't talk above a whisper for over three months. She went to the Holy Spirit weekend where she had met Bernie on the previous course and someone (her hairdresser!) had a word for her about fear (it was fear about never being able to speak or sing in worship again), then he prayed for her. In the morning she woke and found herself humming a worship song! Her voice had been completely restored, so that when Ross [Debs' father] called from Singapore that night and she answered, he thought it was Hannah because he hadn't heard Debs' voice all those months!

Praise our great, miracle-working God!

11

DARING TO COME ALIVE

We make a difference by dreams. All world shapers are dreamers.
They see things in the soft haze of a spring day or in the red fire
of a long winter's evening. Some of us let these dreams die, but
others nourish and protect them; nurse them through bad days
till they bring them to the sunshine and light which comes always
to those who hope that their dreams will come true. No man that
does not see visions will ever realize any high hope or undertake
any high enterprise.

Woodrow Wilson, 28th US President

Much to teach us
23 January 2004

A friend called Pete visited Burundi with Tearfund and sent
back the following report:

As I prayed, I pictured the young woman we had seen, lying in
a pool of her own blood, having just been hit and killed by a car
outside the hospital. She was due to be married on Saturday.
I recalled us talking with a traumatized priest, Father Wilfred,

who explained he had buried seventeen neighbors, all from the same house, in the hole created by the rebel shell that had killed them just three months previously. Father Wilfred showed us his church riddled with bullets. He persuaded the rebels he should stay with them. He said that if he was to die, he wanted to die in his church, but he stayed for seven days burying lots of rebel soldiers instead. We heard of many (so-called) rebel soldiers who were just 13 to 15 years old, child-soldiers. They had had their ear drums destroyed by pouring petrol in their ears and setting light to it, just so they could walk through gunfire, right up to the Government forces, with no fear, firing rounds as they walked into a hail of oncoming gunfire...

Nevertheless, the Bujumbura people we met were full of joy and laughter. They had discovered that each day was to be enjoyed, for who knows what would happen tomorrow. The war-stricken country of Burundi has much to teach us back in the Western world.

Looking back
6 April 2004

Ten years ago today the Rwandan presidential plane was shot down as it came in to land at Kigali airport, killing both the Rwandan and Burundian presidents and precipitating the most clinical and "effective" genocide of recent times, with around 1 million faceless "unpeople" being hacked to death with machetes in the ensuing three months. Among the dead were many family members of those who are now my friends. I was a carefree university student at the time, blissfully unaware of what was taking place, happily drinking, clubbing and playing lots of sport, whilst in Central Africa next-door neighbors turned on each other and, in extreme cases, even killed members of their own family who belonged to the other ethnic group. For me, ignorance was indeed bliss.

But now, ten years on, this part of the world has become part of my very essence. My inner being grieves, groans and yearns for lasting peace, knowing just a fragment of how much people have suffered and are still suffering in these parts. Thankfully, things are looking much more positive in terms of potential lasting peace – more of that below...

It's been great to be back in Burundi for a couple of weeks and link up with so many close friends with whom I have shared both highs and lows, laughter and tears. Last year, for example, I said goodbye to Jean, falsely imprisoned and dying of AIDS. He wouldn't tell people it was AIDS, though, because of the stigma attached to it. He weighed 40 kg and knew he was dying. He rejoiced at the prospect of imminent death and his graduation to glory, and his infectious joy and assurance of heaven drew many others to Christ. However, over the last year two people came to him and told him that God had revealed to them that he indeed had AIDS, but that he would be healed from it for a purpose. He claimed his healing and when I went to visit people in Mpimba prison, I was met by a chubby-cheeked, cheery-faced 70 kg Jean, busy preaching and teaching at the prisoners' improvised Bible school!

My faith is constantly challenged on so many levels by the believers out here. One friend, Gertrude, was praying and fasting with a few others for forty days. On the thirty-first day they were praying through the night when the police came and had them arrested on suspicion of being rebels and planning an insurgency. They were locked up indefinitely. Gertrude was upbeat and insisted it was all part of God's plan, so the group carried on praising God and preaching in the jail, and twenty-six fellow prisoners became Christians, as well as three of the hardened guards. She's now been released but she knows that whatever happens to her, the gospel remains unchained!

I have just returned from an eventful weekend up-country with the SU team. We drove up into the hills to Ngozi, past many former rebels who are now being integrated into the army. It was ironic to see these young rebels who used to hate and kill the Government soldiers, now standing side by side with them (but in a different uniform), and hopefully now protecting us as opposed to ambushing us, as was their wont in the bad old days.

We held a number of meetings in churches and at the university, talking to several thousand people and seeing many respond. Returning on Sunday afternoon, I was driving the minibus in the rain and mud and hit a tree trunk lying in the road. We bounced into the air, everyone screamed "Jeeesuus!" and we landed on the bank, dangling over the edge of the hill. After a few seconds of stunned silence we gingerly got out, as there was a real possibility of the bus rolling off the edge and down the ravine. The damage to the vehicle was minimal, fortunately, but now it really was a race against time because the roads would be closing at 4 p.m. until the following morning, on safety grounds. We took it in turns to dig in the mud and eventually, once a crowd had gathered, twenty men volunteered to try to lift and drag the minibus back onto the road. It took a while, but eventually they managed it, to rapturous applause. Afterwards, we sped onwards for the remaining two hours home, getting stuck twice more in the mud, but beating the road closure by ten minutes. We sang praises to God all the way back in gratitude to Him for His protection and with joy for the privilege of serving Him.

It has been thrilling to see our SU team on fire in all its activities around the country. It has exploded into the fastest-growing and most active Christian group in the land, having been functionally bankrupt just five years ago. There is a new boss called Etienne who is superb, and everyone is highly motivated and passionate. I cannot over-endorse them. The next challenge is consolidation and sustainability, since they are almost entirely dependent on my contacts to finance the work, which I find a crushing responsibility at times. In conjunction with SU, Lizzie and I have agreed to five more years of involvement, after which they must have found their own ways of financing the work. This simply was not possible with the war waging around us over the last few years, but peace is so very close.

With this in mind, we are planning to buy some land in the capital and build a conference center so that profits can be recycled into SU's work to provide long-term sustainability. I believe 100 per cent in what we are doing. Working with the youth of the country nationwide is so strategic, especially when you further consider our AIDS project and our involvement with street children and orphans.

The transitional Government will end in six months' time and so, as the new elections approach, these are critical times for Burundi. The war has been going on for over a decade and peace has never been closer, but there are plenty of factions vying for power, so we're not out of the woods yet.

Absurd dreams
6 September 2004

> There are some people who live in a dream world, and there are some who face reality; and then there are those who turn one into the other.
>
> **Douglas Everett**

I am challenged by the above quote because, although I dream of peace in Burundi and Congo, the obstacles in the battle for lasting peace often appear insurmountable. Yet, through the eyes of faith, and facing up to the grim realities on the ground, with costly and concerted perseverance we will see war turned to peace.

There are seven weeks to go until the deadline runs out for elections to take place. They will be the first elections since those eleven years ago which led to the genocide. Things are hotting up and these are crucial times. Similar to last week's horrific school massacre in Russia, a few weeks ago saw renewed mindless violence just 10 km from the capital. Here is one of the emails I received from a colleague about what happened:

> I like to inform you that I was in sad state from last Friday,
> 13 August 2004. I hear about Congolese refugees in Burundi
> was been victims of attack of groups of killers and Congolese
> soldiers who come from Uvira valley to Burundi where our
> people was and they kill 163 victims, women, babies, children,
> men, because they are Tutsi. And 200 injured who are dying
> every day in Burundi hospitals. In that number of victims our
> family's members are 53 people who are victims of that genocide
> still continuing from Congo until Burundi. I don't know how to
> explain we are in sad state. Pray for us and our relatives. God
> bless you.

The massacre took place right where I have often preached. Machetes, grenades and guns were used. Two of the children who were killed were in the process of being reintegrated into their families from one of the orphanages we are connected with.

The new lady in charge of the UN mission arrived. She sounds like a good person. She declared on the radio:

> The Burundian women have suffered enormously. I have heard
> the stories of what happens to women alone in Burundi when
> they try to flee to go to the refugee camps. They get raped as they
> try to flee, they get raped when they cross the border, they get
> raped on the way to the camps, and they get raped when they try

to collect firewood. If they come back and discover that they are also under attack from the very people who have come here to save them, this is more than [adding] insult to injury: it is a crime. And it will not happen, I will not tolerate it in Burundi.

Another group of friends traveling in convoy was ambushed on a road I regularly use. They were stripped, forced to hand over all their possessions, had their vehicles torched, and then other troops arrived and there was a battle. Everyone managed to jump into the bushes and got away with their lives. So, things are *chaud* (hot), as they say out there.

I read today of a little fellow in the slum who was being teased by another boy: "If God loves you, why doesn't he take care of you?" he taunted. "Why doesn't God tell someone to bring you shoes and a warm coat and better food?" The little lad thought for a moment, then, with tears welling in his eyes, replied, "I guess He does tell somebody, but somebody forgets." May none of us be the "somebody" who forgets.

I just heard by email about little Bongani, my orphan buddy with AIDS whose dream was to see the sea before he died. After a plucky fight, he died last month, aged eleven. He is one among millions of victims of this disease. But his life did count and his story has touched many lives. I will never forget him.

Come alive
16 November 2004

After our first year of marriage spent in the UK, Lizzie and I are now well and truly back in Burundi. We've been here just a few weeks and I've written some reflections in an update to send out to our friends:

What makes you come alive? I have just read the following:

> Don't ask yourself what the world needs. Ask yourself what
> makes you come alive, and go do that, because what the world
> needs is people who have come alive... Sanctified resignation
> has become the new abiding place of contemporary Christians...
> Christianity has come to the point where we believe that there
> is no higher aspiration for the human soul than to be nice. We
> are producing a generation of men and women whose greatest
> virtue is that they don't offend anyone. Then we wonder why
> there is not more passion for Christ. How can we hunger and
> thirst for righteousness if we have ceased hungering and thirsting
> altogether?
>
> **John Eldredge, *Wild at Heart***

I am back in the land which makes me come alive. Ironically, it is a land of death, disease, injustice and pain, and yet it is a land which sets my pulse racing and fills me with passion and raw energy as I seek to live out what the Lord has called me to do. The needs are endless, the stories are heartbreaking, the pain is palpable, but the believers cling to their God and see His faithfulness in the face of extreme difficulties.

A few days after Lizzie and I arrived back in Burundi, we went out for what we thought was just supper with a few friends, but it turned out to be a surprise party for our return. It was also a late wedding celebration, because all of them couldn't be at our wedding last year in England.

As we entered the Youth for Christ premises, fifty people cheered and clapped while the troupe of trained street children unleashed their pounding arms onto twelve goatskin drums and pranced theatrically around the compound. The noise was deafening, the atmosphere intensely alive. As we ate together, I looked around at the faces of many extraordinary brothers and sisters with whom I have shared both powerful and dangerous times over the last several years.

I have just returned from a few days' evangelism in the bush. These weekends are what make me come alive the most, as they are tiring, bonding, exciting, unpredictable, smelly, uncomfortable, varied, fruitful, etc., usually with freezing showers and no electricity. YFC had done some fantastic work a few months ago with street children in the town. So this time I met the leader of the street gangs, who had been one of the top crooks, but now helps our SU staff run a literacy class. It made me think that Jesus truly is the One who transforms and makes people come alive, because he is The Life.

We had several meetings and saw many people come to the Lord. The harvest is plentiful in this land and the battle is obvious on many levels. New minarets are springing up all over the place and I am woken up regularly by the call to prayer, especially at this time towards the end of the fasting month of Ramadan. On the way back we came across yet another Jehovah's Witness kingdom hall. People are spiritually hungry and we sense an urgency in telling them about how they can *really* come alive.

The peace process is juddering on. The elections have been forcibly postponed until next April because the constitution had not been ratified in time and few people are optimistic. However, the countryside has a feeling of peace about it. Ambushes are rare at the moment; there is only sporadic shooting and we feel very safe on the roads up-country.

Lizzie is settling in well and getting stuck into language study, which is often frustrating. It's wonderful to have her here with me. My colleagues and friends love her already. I have been told repeatedly, "Simon, we are so happy to see you with Madame. Before you were just an *umuhungu* [a boy], but now you are an *umugabo* [a man]!" We're looking for permanent accommodation whilst staying in some friends' annex (which was a great answer to prayer in itself).

The needs continue to be overwhelming at times, but we trust in God. The psalmist says, "Delight yourself in the Lord, and he will give you the desires of your heart" (Psalm 37:4). There is nothing like following The Life, who offers each one of us in our respective situations life to the full. Dear God, help us to say no to "sanctified resignation" and to aspiring to being "nice" or inoffensive. Rather, help us to come truly alive to meet the needs of a desperate and dying world. "Only one life, 'twill soon be past. Only what's done for Christ will last." (attributed to C. T. Studd).

Weakness

7 December 2004

I've mostly spent the last few days in bed. I've been to the hospital again and am undergoing a second treatment for malaria, although tests don't show anything apart from some residual typhoid. I'm so weak. Lizzie has been a star pampering me, yet at times I'm deeply discouraged. I've finished a study in bed on Job (ironically or appropriately) and was hoping that as I finished it, I would be restored – cheeky to compare myself to him, I know! But Job learnt a great deal about trusting the sovereign plans of the Lord, so hopefully I can too. Maybe God will throw in loads of beautiful daughters at the end as well!

It's interesting that this sickness kicked in straight after a fruitful weekend of evangelism in the bush, seeing God's kingdom of light pierce the darkness, and also straight after I vowed to get up regularly at 6 a.m. to pray. I'm not saying there is an automatic link, but it was only last week I read something like this:

> Just see how much Satan hates our prayers by deciding to
> really pray seriously for a two-week period. You'll be amazed

what happens to you immediately to knock you off your perch. Suddenly things go wrong or something unexpected happens and the Enemy will try anything to keep you from your good intentions.

This reminds me that we are in a constant battle.

Blessed suffering
12 December 2004

I woke up and stayed awake from 4 a.m. today. At 4.30 there were three loud gunshots just outside. It must have been thieves. It's unnerving to think that someone may have died as the echoes of the bullets reverberate for several seconds. Having said that, this is the quietest period in recent times in the country.

This was my twelfth day sick in bed. Whilst Lizzie was at church I lay in bed and really felt the Lord speaking to me and giving me lots of ideas. This time of bodily inactivity has seen heightened brain activity and communion with Him, with time to redefine my purpose and vision and sharpen areas of ministry. In retrospect, I can see that it would not have been such a significant time spiritually had I been fit, healthy and *busy doing stuff* for God (like He really needs me to anyway!). Blessed suffering! I've hated it, but I begrudgingly thank God for it. He is a wise, loving Heavenly Father.

I watched a video on the genocide in Rwanda, and the utter moral bankruptcy, inactivity, obfuscation and ineptitude of the international community astounded me afresh. "Never again" was declared with contrition, and yet the same big players are similarly minimizing active involvement in Darfur right now, and in the Congo, and in other places. I heard on the radio that the International Red Cross have produced a report estimating that 1,000 people are dying each day in

Congo from the conflict. That's the equivalent of two 9/11s each week! Aid per individual in Iraq is $180, whereas in Congo it is a meager $3.23.

What a sick, out-of-balance world we live in.

12

HALFWAY AND BEYOND

Live ready. If you have to get ready when the opportunity comes
your way, you'll be too late. Opportunity doesn't wait, not even
while you pray. You must not have to get ready, you must live
ready at all times.

Smith Wigglesworth

Witchcraft for real?
31 January 2005

I recently became friends with Saleh and I felt his story would
challenge the world view of many who read it, so I sent it out
to our prayer team:

Do you believe in witchcraft? Sorcery? Demons? Satanic
power? I wonder what you make of this:

Recently, I had a much-anticipated visit from Saleh, a
converted Muslim sheikh. He shared with me his extraordinary
story. He was born into a Christian family, but educated away
from home and became a Muslim when he was fourteen years
old. He was initiated into folk Islamic practices involving

sorcery. The higher he rose in Islam, the more witchcraft he got caught up in. To obtain satanic powers he engaged in bestiality, made evil potions and created blood bonds with people (I'll spare the details). As a result he was able to woo almost any woman he wanted and used his powers to bewitch a Christian lady in the church choir, whom he married. She would pray for him, but he was always alerted through his satanic powers when she was praying, and would interrupt and warn her that he would kill her if she carried on.

He became very rich because he could take whatever he wanted from shops by blinding the owners of the shops he visited. Indeed, my friend Lin, who led Saleh to Christ and who brought him along to see me, told me how they went shopping together, and it was only long after leaving the shops that Lin's own eyes were opened to seeing all the stuff Saleh had stolen. He had been blinded as well! But Saleh was tormented by evil spirits (called *jinn*) at night. He talked of walking into the lake and traveling into another world where he would meet demons and do all kinds of things with them. On one occasion under the lake, the demons told him to rip up the Bible, which he refused to do, so the demons said he would die poor as a result.

He returned to Bujumbura and his father prayed for him because he was particularly crazy or possessed after his under-lake-world experience. He rejected the exorcism and fled up-country, but his interest in Christ and his confusion over Islam pushed him to investigate Christianity. He had a Jehovah's Witness friend and when they met up the latter derided Christ ("Jesus was a sinner, He didn't even get married… what's so special about Him, then?"). That was on a Friday. The man dropped dead two days later on Sunday. Saleh saw that his friend had cursed Jesus and then died, so he concluded that Jesus must be very powerful. To cut a long story short, he asked for Lin's help. A team of people prayed and fasted for three days before exorcising all the demons in Jesus' name.

Saleh was totally transformed. When the *jinn* appeared at night to threaten him, he rebuked them in Jesus' name and they have never returned. He then went back to shops to make restitution for what he had stolen. That was five years ago. Since then he has lost all his wealth, been ostracized and threatened and now has a job as a primary school teacher earning just $20 per month. He has memorized the Scriptures and is a man steeped in prayer. I asked him what it was like to lose everything. He sighed, smiled and said, "Now I have peace in my heart. Jesus has set me free. That is worth more than all the wealth I had before."

Saleh wants to go public with his story now that he is more spiritually equipped and mature, and I asked him if he was willing to be killed if we went ahead and distributed tapes of his testimony, which will undoubtedly be circulated far and wide and have a massive impact. He said that first he would fast and pray for twenty-one days to prepare himself for the inevitable battles which would ensue. He has a wife and three children to think of. He is taking huge risks and it is not a decision to be taken lightly.

Sometimes it's good to hear someone's story that doesn't fit into our neat boxes, and one which highlights the spiritual battle we are all involved in. It illustrates the power of the name of Jesus and how critical prayer, fasting, and knowing the Word of God are to us. We face the same enemy in the West, although he is much more subtle in his attempts to lead us astray. Indeed, materialism, relativism, spiritual apathy and general busyness seem far more effective weapons than such blatant attacks as the one recounted above. So let's get praying!

Having spent much of the last two months in bed, I'm now back in the UK. Despite having seen the best specialist in the country, we still don't know what it is which has wiped me out. Nothing has shown up in detailed tests. Humanly speaking, we have tried everything. Could it be witchcraft, some kind of spell? Maybe you think I'm being daft. Who knows? But how short-sighted of the devil, because this experience has undoubtedly drawn me closer to the Lord and has enabled me to spend invaluable and highly fruitful time strategizing, planning and writing a book.

Lizzie has been amazing. She has continued on in Burundi by herself and we have been apart for nearly a month now. I am so proud of her and how she has settled in and been embraced by those around her. We both thank God for how easy the transition has been for her to adapt to Burundi and we are very grateful to those who have prayed for us. I can't wait to see her when she flies over this week. Then she will join me in the US for some important preaching opportunities. Our trip is both an exciting and a daunting prospect for me in my current state. I do believe it will be a significant time, however, as it has been much prayed over and prepared for.

Some verses I have memorized of late that carry particular significance, since I am feeling so weak, are Paul's words in 2 Corinthians 12:8–10:

> Three times I pleaded with the Lord to take [the thorn in my flesh] away from me. But he said to me, 'My grace is sufficient for you, for my power is made perfect in weakness." Therefore I will boast all the more gladly about my weaknesses, so that Christ's power may rest on me... For when I am weak, then I am strong.

Please pray for healing, energy and, as the passage says, for Christ's power to rest on me, so that many people will be deeply impacted with the gospel.

Back to the Book
16 March 2005

Two quotes have struck me recently, one by a Muslim, the other by a Hindu:

Ayatollah Fadlallah, the spiritual leader of the Islamic fundamentalist group Hezbollah in Lebanon, said to Brother Andrew: "You Christians have a problem."

The latter enquired, "What do you think our problem is?"

Fadlallah replied, "You are not following the life of Jesus Christ any more."

Andrew asked again, "So what do you think we should do about that?"

"You must go back to the Book," came the reply.

Referring to the Bible, Mahatma Gandhi said to a group of missionaries, "You Christians look after a document containing enough dynamite to blow all civilization to pieces, turn the world upside down and bring peace to a battle-torn planet. But you treat it as though it is nothing more than a piece of literature."

God help us truly to follow the life of Jesus Christ, to get back to the Book, to take hold of this spiritual dynamite and be taken hold of, such that we do turn the world upside down and help bring peace to our battle-torn planet!

A girl on our SU youth camp was on her way to blow up her mum, dad and sisters' killers with a grenade. She was touched by the Lord and brought out the grenade, confessed and repented in Jesus' name. That's the power of the gospel!

Last week a lad tracked us down at SU to say that after our last camp, when people prayed for his mum whose hand had been withered for many years, he returned home to find her healed. He had searched for SU for ages to share this great news. Wherever we go, we constantly hear from people telling us that they gave their lives to the Lord during our last visit, or at a meeting in some other part of the country. It is thrilling to be a part of God's work out here.

I visited Mount Pleasant, South Carolina, on my trip to the US – the second time I'd been out there. After two months of being sick in bed in Burundi and then the UK, and having undergone all possible tests without result, the Lord healed me just in time to go and preach over thirty times during a manic few weeks. Lizzie joined me for part of it and we shared at all sorts of meetings. It was hectic, but great fun. We experienced incredible hospitality and friendliness and got to meet a whole bunch of wonderful people.

Returning from beautiful, opulent Mount Pleasant to the extreme poverty of Burundi, I struggled, yet again, to reconcile the fact that we are living on the same planet. How can we believers in the West justify the lavish excess of our lifestyles when our brothers and sisters can't even afford essential medicine or food? I don't write that in order to make anyone feel guilty – it is something that genuinely fries my brain. The number of children dying of preventable diseases in sub-Saharan Africa is equivalent to having one Asian tsunami *every week*! The world is so unfair. We like to retain a certain level of ignorance about these things, because that way we don't have to address the issues.

One of the most powerful lines from the Oscar-nominated film *Hotel Rwanda* comes when the US journalist has managed to get some live footage of people hacking others to death. The Rwandan hotel manager says something like, "You must show it to the world and then they will come and stop this mass murder." But the journalist replies, "The truth is, people will probably say, 'Oh my God' and then carry on eating their supper." In fact, upwards of 800,000 people *were* systematically hacked to death while we (myself included) carried on eating our supper.

On the political scene, praise God that the referendum took place peacefully two weeks ago. Elections are due in the next few months. As the last elections in 1993 precipitated the genocide of over 150,000 people, this is a very big deal. The church has a huge role to play and we need to be united.

I return to Fadlallah's and Gandhi's words... I take those rebukes on the chin and vow to live passionately and wholeheartedly, surrendering everything for Christ's sake. After all, how far is too far when He went so far?

Halfway and beyond
10 May 2005

Johannes Eckhart, a fifteenth-century mystic, wrote: "There are plenty of Christians to follow the Lord halfway, but not the other half. They will give up possessions, friends, and honors, but it touches them too closely to disown themselves."

Hmm... Well, here's to moving towards the halfway mark and beyond! Over the last few weeks I have been preaching up-country with a number of people who counted the cost and were prepared to give up possessions, friends, and honors, and even to disown themselves:

Pastor Juvenal was the only man in his whole area to refuse to "contribute" financially to his tribe's rebel cause. He also preached from the pulpit that church members should not side with the rebellion or resort to armed conflict. Consequently, the rebels came on a number of occasions to kill him. However, as with the martyrs of Revelation 12:11 who "did not love their lives so much as to shrink from death", he was prepared to disown himself and die. He survived many close shaves.

Recently, with the disbanding of that rebel group, the

commander who had tried to kill him sought him out and shook his hand, saying, "Congratulations! Truly you are a man of God. We tried to get you and were determined to kill you, but God always protected you!" The commander invited Juvenal to the demobilization camp to preach to several thousand troops who were duly amazed to see the famous rebellious pastor still alive! Many of them repented and turned to Christ.

Then there was Ephraim, who runs our SU northern office. He was returning by foot to Burundi after a year as a refugee in the Congo. He felt he simply had to get back to his homeland, but soldiers from the other tribe took him and tortured him. He told them that God was calling him back to Burundi and so they could try to kill him, but he knew his time had not yet come to die. They just thought he was mad. But as they attempted to kick him to death he told them that he forgave them and loved them in Jesus' name. They left him for dead in a crumpled heap, pouring with blood. However, he revived and is now being used extraordinarily in the schools and churches around Ngozi. "That was the day I learned what real forgiveness is about," he told me.

Two weeks ago Pierre preached with me at a dilapidated church situated in an area in the hills decimated by the war – its devastation contrasting with the stunning view across the lake to the majestic Congolese mountains. The month before a group of ladies had been praying in the church when the mud walls caved in on them. Thankfully, none of them died. Now they are rebuilding. Pierre said in a matter-of-fact way, "Soldiers killed my father who was the pastor and two of my brothers. But Simon, when you have Jesus, it's OK."

How these people challenge and humble me as I consider my own cushioned existence, self-absorption, petty grievances and fickle faith! I have never plumbed the depths of human grief that almost everyone out here has, so how can I really understand? What do I really know? Who do I think I am, urging them to forgive those who raped or butchered their loved ones? Such are the questions I ask myself as I stand before people to share the Word of God, feeling suitably inadequate to the task. Nevertheless, they accept and embrace me and the team, particularly as they know we are amongst the few who have risked traveling through such dangerous areas over the last few years, willing to die to bring them the life-giving message of Christ.

We had some friends out to visit for a couple of weeks and took a road trip to Lake Kivu in Rwanda, which is where I proposed to Lizzie two and a half years ago. As Lizzie drove the truck, with Mark and I in the back lying on top of our luggage and enjoying the sunshine, an impatient car pulled up close behind and beeped aggressively, wanting to overtake on the narrow section of road. Lizzie duly clattered through a pothole with a fresh cowpat in it and sprayed the driver as well as a bunch of soldiers who were jogging past. That was the biggest laugh I've had in a long time. The moral of the story, which I've already learnt the hard way, is don't get on the wrong side of Lizzie Guillebaud!

Following Jesus is so very exciting, fulfilling, challenging, gutting, exasperating, discouraging, exhausting, thrilling and *real*! Here's to not settling or stopping halfway, but going all the way!

13

AN EFFORTLESS
INTIMACY?

Do you tend more to striving or abiding? Is your striving a
joyful reflection of God's grace and your abiding a disciplined
communion with Christ?

Meg Foote

The best insurance policy
22 June 2005

Right now I have a fantastic team from South Carolina visiting
and joining me in the work here, so we enjoyed the day with
the street kids down at the beach swimming in the lake with
a hippo nearby. Later we shared testimonies during a deeply
humbling and moving time together. Before we'd left for the
beach that morning, many of us had listened with tears in our
eyes as the founder of New Generation (recently awarded a
prize as the best youth organization in Africa), Dieudonné,
recounted how he had begun the work a decade ago when
someone felt sorry for him and gave him $5.

It was Christmas Day 1993 when it all started. His father had just been thrown, still alive, into a pit and then covered over. Dieudonné felt terribly alone and destitute, with seemingly nobody and nothing in the world. But then he walked past some street children and realized, with the small amount of money he'd been given, that he had $5 more than them at least, so he bought some sodas and shared the message of Christmas with them. Slowly but surely things have grown in the intervening years and he now has sixty-four children in his care. Last year he was able to return to the scene of his father's murder and preach about forgiveness and reconciliation. He showed us a photo of him with one of the group responsible for killing his father.

He also spoke of a day when they were all going hungry as a group. As they prayed they asked the Lord to provide for them, but not just with someone else's scraps. Rather, in faith they asked the Lord to provide them with an amazing meal. At that very moment elsewhere in the capital, I was leaving an embassy function at which there was tray after tray of delicacies. Everything that was left over was going to be thrown away, so I asked if I could take the food for the street children. A few minutes later I arrived at New Generation's office to hand over the Ambassador of Britain's food to these cute, little, hungry, faith-filled Ambassadors for Christ! How amazing it is to see God work like this.

Through the years these little urchins have constantly seen the Lord answer their heartfelt pleas, "Give us today our daily bread," and that is how Dieudonné wants to continue. Recently, a major donor pulled out and he has just emailed me to say they have been kicked out of their house with no money to move elsewhere. Things are a real struggle for them just now, but they continue to trust God.

Lizzie and I have also needed to trust Him all the more at this time, as Lizzie is going through a difficult pregnancy. She is approaching four months and a few weeks ago we thought we had lost the budding little Bilbo Gilbo (my nickname for the bump – I think it's got a good ring to it!). After some bleeding, cramps and a pessimistic initial diagnosis from the doctor, Lizzie has been confined to bed-rest and is flying back to the UK earlier than planned. We're still hopeful that a feisty nipper will pop out sometime in December.

I am writing this at a seminar up-country in Rumonge, as one of the team in front of me is teaching a group of church leaders. A number of the pastors invited have not been able to attend because a group of vigilante guards demanding payment have set up roadblocks around the city and are not letting people through. Things have been tense. Updates on the situation are being given hourly on national radio. Indeed, as I write this, forty armed soldiers have just stomped past to go and try to break up the demonstration. We are hoping to be able to get back to the capital after lunch in a few hours.

I came across a challenging quote last week: "The biblical images to describe the work of the Spirit – fire, mighty rushing wind, flood etc. – are exactly the sorts of things we pay to insure ourselves against." May God help us to make Him our Insurance Policy – and nobody or nothing else!

Simple fools

24 August 2005

These are potentially historic times for Burundi! Imagine listening to shells landing and bullets being fired, on and off, for the last twelve years. Rape and pillage have been routine experiences for many, including plenty of my friends. Twelve years is a long time. But God's people have continued crying out to Him, clinging to their hope in Him, reaching out to the lost for Him. And, many years and many tears later, our hopes are rising. Freddy just wrote to me:

Peter Nkurunziza has been elected as the new President of Burundi with 91.5 per cent of the votes. When he was asked to say something to the nation after the elections, he thanked God first – he actually prayed. The second thing he did was to thank God's servants. We believe he will lead nicely our nation. We're so thankful to God for what He is doing in Burundi. This is going to be a new chapter in this nation where people are both physically and spiritually hungry. As I am writing this message I hear voices of people singing – we're having an all-night prayer meeting at our office. We fully believe that things are going to change here in Burundi.

Indeed, these are exciting days for Burundi. The obstacles still remain huge, however, with one rebel movement refusing to lay down weapons. Another eight people were killed just outside the capital the other day in an attack. The poverty is crippling, famine continues in the North and banditry is on the rise. The new President needs so much prayer. He has an onerous task ahead of him – it's a poisoned chalice, almost – with all of his predecessors ending up murdered. Yet, he has called on God's help and so will we.

Other great news is that the team from the States a few months ago proved to be the catalyst for a mini-revival on the main university campus, with twenty-five students giving their lives to the Lord at the extraordinary meeting we convened. That was followed by a national student congress a few weeks later, to which far more came than were invited, and the result has been a massive groundswell of support for the movement with people re-envisioned, mobilized, equipped and sent back on fire to all the campuses around the country. This is all the more important as our Muslim neighbors are strategically targeting the universities.

I love being a part of this incredible adventure. I read these words by Pete Greig the other day:

The eyes of the Lord are still searching out those willing to live their lives above the gunnels of mediocrity and beyond the realms of inevitability. In our cynical age, God is looking for those naïve enough to believe that the world can still be changed, those simple fools whose vision is to live and die for Christ alone.

Pete Greig, *The Vision and the Vow*

Call me naïve or a simple fool, but here's to living and dying for Christ alone!

Praying Hyde
25 September 2005

After a couple of months of preaching around the UK and USA, I have just returned to Burundi by myself, leaving Lizzie in England until the birth of little Bilbo Gilbo in December. They both seem in great shape, growing more pronounced by the day. This separation is not ideal and of course I miss them, but being on my own has been very different from what I expected.

I hesitate to write the following, at the risk of sounding super-spiritual, but I haven't experienced such intimacy with God since I first came out here seven years ago. Back then I was twenty-five, had left everything, and arrived in this crazy country having been robbed of most of my money. Miscommunication and confusion meant my role was unclear. I knew virtually nobody, was relatively clueless, and yet it was an incredible time of dependence on the Lord, who answered my urgent prayers with extraordinary interventions. I remember being so full of the joy of the Holy Spirit that people would laugh at me, because I was overflowing with Him. I would go into my room and feel totally overcome. I would sing for joy and feel like I was going to explode. While I was desperate, weak and vulnerable, I was being forced to depend on Him and it was actually a glorious dependence. I took big risks and He was faithful all the way – it was the adventure of living I was created for. I have often since harkened back to those precious times.

As with all pilgrimages, however, mountain-top experiences are followed by valleys, and lush pastures by arid deserts. The last seven years have been undeniably fruitful and exciting, but preaching a hundred times a year has sometimes left me stale and sapped of spiritual vigor. Now, this week, I have had a new visitation. It has been an amazing time. I only write a little about it, because maybe there is something we can learn from each other's journeys.

As I said goodbye to Lizzie and her parents at the airport, my dearest Mum was being cut open to have her gall-bladder and a cancerous growth in her colon removed. It was a bad time to leave. I had loads of excess luggage and could have been fined a few hundred pounds, but we prayed and the lady at the counter let me off the hook. I had a long conversation with a lovely Hindu on the plane who said that he preferred Christianity to Hinduism! I shared the gospel with him and he said he wanted forgiveness of sins and assurance of heaven through Jesus, but was not quite ready. I gave him my details and I hope I will hear from him.

I'm reading the biography of John Nelson Hyde, the American missionary to India who became known to the world as "Praying Hyde", and it is so challenging. As I tried to emulate him by throwing myself passionately into prayer for hours on my bed in the dark, it suddenly struck me that these two months will probably be my quietest for the next few decades! So instead of bemoaning my loneliness, this could be the most fabulous time of nurturing intimacy with the Lord by spending as much time with Him as possible. Generally, I'm not good at being solely in my own company, but I have loved the chance to pray undisturbed tonight – not something I could do easily during the hectic travel of the past few months. Lord, I give you this time and surrender my life afresh. Have your way and do whatever you want with me.

Since then I have been up praying at 6 a.m. each morning and have been free most evenings from 7 p.m. onwards to spend hours praying, belting out songs of praise and adoration on the guitar, seeking His face and interceding for the lost. It has blown me away.

Effortless intimacy?
27 September 2005

Today was fasting day. I felt caught up in an extraordinary state – a mountain-top experience. It surely has to do with the fact that I am spending so much time in the Lord's presence. What a numbskull I am and how slow to learn the fact that intimacy, which we all crave, can only be attained and sustained through disciplined commitment and time given to Him. *We want effortless intimacy, but it just doesn't happen that way.*

I was up at the crack of dawn and jumped out of bed with a, "Good morning, Jesus!" I am full of gratitude that Mum's cancer operation has been declared a success. I prayed passionately, sang, read the Bible, and then started preparing a sermon to preach at Sunday's International Fellowship. I wanted to make notes on the computer, but it seemed like it had fused with the latest power cut. The power wouldn't go on, although everything else electrical was working. I prayed over the computer and went off to start searching the Scriptures for the right message. I came back to find it working and the sermon flowed out as never before! I could hear the Lord so clearly, the ideas and structure came so easily. Truly, the preparation of the messenger is as important as the preparation of the message.

God knows how long this season of extraordinary intimacy will last, but in any case I want to maximize it, keep up the discipline and guard the time spent in His presence. I mustn't let busyness crowd Him out. It is so obvious and we all know prayer is of paramount importance, but Satan will do anything to distract us from what renders him powerless.

A holy inconvenience
30 September 2005

Whilst I was in the bath in the evening, Bruno (from three houses along) came to visit. I sent him away, but knew he would be around again shortly. Instead of viewing him as a nuisance who wants to learn English and use up my valuable time, I chose to view him as someone sent by God to come to faith through me. I claimed his life for Jesus and interceded on his behalf. Before reading the *Praying Hyde* book, I would have just prayed a fifteen-second-prayer: "Right, Lord, Bruno is coming round. Please open the eyes of his heart to see you, and give me the right words to say. May he come to know you, Amen." Instead, I really prayed and spent serious time at it, putting off supper until I had done so. I worshipped away on the guitar and proclaimed the Lord's victory until my fingers were just too sore to carry on.

Then Bruno showed up again. He's a nice lad, about twenty-two years old. We chatted about football, school etc., and then I asked him if he would say he was a Christian – was he ready to face judgment? I went through the gospel and asked him if he wanted to receive Christ as his Lord and Savior right now. "No pressure," I told him, "but do you want to be ready?" He told me he did. I prayed and he repeated the words after me. He's coming with me to church on Sunday. We will hook up and regularly read a passage from the Bible together. Seal your work in his life, O Lord!

Just on time
12 October 2005

I've decided with a heavy heart to be hard on Dieudonné, because he owes me personally a lot of money and yet he keeps coming to me to rescue him. He busts a gut to provide for eighty street children whom he simply cannot abandon. He's a superb man of God, and there are few people on earth who I respect more, but we need to see a breakthrough. I'm praying in desperation for this situation. Our last conversation still weighs on my mind. It's hard to say no, but he must learn to look to God and not to me to bail him out. Meanwhile, the kids and he are all going hungry and not going to school. He rang again late this morning and ended up pleading with me for $10. He sounded broken, stressed, tired and discouraged. He was just phoning from the street and had nothing left. It was a painful conversation. I said I was in prayer for him that God would bail him out with a miracle of provision today. I felt heartless on the one hand, but I told him I would be fasting with them and we will rejoice when we see the Lord intervene and confirm the fact that it is His work for His glory.

Now it's 10 p.m. I've checked my emails for the last time, having asked the Lord to provide the answer before the day is over, *and there it is – a gift of $900 for Dieudonné's work*! It is just what he needs with all his debts. *Hallelujah!* I love the life of faith! God, you are awesome! I can go to bed now with a smile on my face. I love you, Jesus!

Too busy to have power
28 October 2005

R. A. Torrey wrote: "We are too busy to pray, and so we are too busy to have power. We have a great deal of activity but we accomplish little; many services but few conversions;

much machinery but few results."

The members of the Punjab Prayer Union (Hyde amongst them), who experienced revival in their midst, had to sign the following declaration to become members. It was in the form of five questions:

1. Are you praying for quickening in your own life, in the life of your fellow-workers, and in the Church?
2. Are you longing for greater power of the Holy Spirit in your own life and work, and are you convinced that you cannot go on without this power?
3. Will you pray that you may not be ashamed of Jesus?
4. Do you believe that prayer is the great means for securing this spiritual awakening?
5. Will you set apart one half-hour each day to pray for this awakening, and are you willing to pray till the awakening comes?

This is so challenging. I know more impacting lessons on prayer are coming my way.

Papa Zac!
17 December 2005

This is just a quick note to say that Lizzie gave birth last night in Southampton after many hours of labor, and out came beautiful little Zac Rocky Guillebaud! He weighed in at 6lb 11oz. Lizzie's very tender, which I am not remotely surprised about, having watched her body contort and stretch in extraordinary ways. It was *amazing* to be part of such a tortuous, painful, exhilarating, scary and miraculous event. I still feel blown away by it.

We immediately dedicated Zac back to the Lord as His gift for His glory. Now maybe we'll have to start behaving like adults!

Here's wishing you a merry and meaningful Christmas. Last night, as Zac eventually entered the world in all that mess, it made me think all the more how powerful the reality of the founder of Christmas' embracing of humanity was – living and dying to bring life to others.

God bless you all,

Papa Zac (as I'll now be called in Burundi!).

14

Joining in God's Story

Either we wake to tackle our "to do" list, get things done, guided by our morals and whatever clarity we may at the moment have. Or we wake in the midst of a Dangerous Story, as God's intimate ally, following Him into the unknown. If you are not pursuing a dangerous quest with your life, well, then, you don't need a Guide. If you haven't found yourself in the midst of a ferocious war, then you won't need a seasoned Captain. If you've settled in your mind to live as though this is a fairly neutral world and you are simply trying to live your life as best you can, then you can probably get by with the Christianity of tips and techniques. Maybe. I'll give you about a fifty-fifty chance. But if you intend to live in the Story that God is telling, and if you want the life He offers, then you are going to need more than a handful of principles, however noble they may be. There are too many twists and turns in the road ahead, too many ambushes waiting only God knows where, too much at stake. You cannot possibly prepare yourself for every situation. Narrow is the way, said Jesus, how shall we be sure to find it? We need God intimately, and we need Him desperately.

John Eldredge

His dangerous story
21 February 2006

What's the story? Although we know that for us it will end happily ever after, it's certainly no fairy tale. It's too messy, painful and ugly at times – be it in Burundi's literal "ferocious war" or your own struggles to live out a relevant and impacting faith in a culture obsessed with Mammon, sex, political correctness and relativism. I guess if we choose to enter into the story that God is telling, rather than insisting on writing our own story, then we won't be sucked and bled dry. We'll have more than a fifty-fifty chance of surviving to tell the tale.

The opening quote makes me think of my friends Tim and Maz, who live in a village near Aylesbury. God recently directed them to give away their most valuable possession, their car, even though they needed it for work and taking their boys to school. In obedience they gave it away to a needy family. They are living a raw, exciting, dangerous journey of faith, trusting God to script His story in their lives for His glory. I love it! (And, of course, within a few days the Lord provided them with a new car from someone they'd never met!) Yes, people can live radical lives of faith in the West – it just means seeking God and stepping out in unsafe, uncomfortable faith, taking risks and daring to believe that God is faithful to His children, because that is His character.

Back to Burundi. What's the story here? Few of us had the faith to believe all sorts of whacky prophecies that were being given in the last few years. For instance, that the next President was going to be a full-on Christian; that peace would come; that poor little Burundi, at the heart of Africa, would end up being a blessing to the rest of the continent. It all seemed a little far-fetched. But back in 1999 a rebel soldier of ordinary rank was shot by the national army in a jungle attack and left for dead by his fleeing companions. He says he was sure he was going to die, but somehow pulled through after four months of being at death's door. During that time he had a powerful encounter with Jesus and a pastor came and prophesied over him that one day he would become President of Burundi. Just a few months ago that seemingly insignificant, former rebel soldier was chosen in democratic elections to be President! I have had a one-on-one meeting with him and he showed me the scar on his leg where he was shot. I think he is the real deal. Time will tell.

The second Deputy President also gave her life to the Lord last month. Can you get excited with me? Now, whether she and the President stay on track or subsequently get killed or corrupted, it's hard to deny that God is on the move and playing His part in response to the years of intercession arising from this blood-stained nation. And please, you can have a part to play in this story too, by praying for Peter Nkurunziza (*nkuru nziza* means "good news"!): that he stays alive (several attempts have already been made on his life), is wise and discerning (he is still a young Christian), remains uncorrupted (in a land of institutionalized corruption), and stays on track spiritually (a number of African heads of state have professed faith in Christ, but have ended up as evil tyrants).

Stable elections and the transition to democratic rule were an incredible blessing and the answer to many prayers, but things are far from perfect. Although nearly every province is now peaceful, around Bujumbura the one remaining rebel faction continues to wreak havoc. Daily there are shootings, people are murdered or raped, and houses are looted. Clarice, who works for us, lives up in the hills and comes in each day with fresh stories of woe from the previous night. She tries to muffle the cries of her traumatized baby so that they are not attacked themselves. Following on from those rebel incursions, reprisals by the army seem arbitrary. A friend's brother was taken as a suspected rebel a few days ago with another young lad. The latter was beaten to death, although innocent. We've got a long way to go in this land.

There is also famine, as bad as it's ever been in my seven years out here. The response to the urgent needs has been slow and inadequate, and many are dying daily. People will resort to eating the bark off trees, or inedible roots and leaves, just to fill their stomachs. It's a grim world where I can stuff my face and throw away leftovers whilst others will pick through the mud to collect a few grains of discarded rice – a sight I once saw, to my shame, after wiping away the last remains of what I considered my "empty" plate.

Petro-dollars from Libya and the Middle East are being pumped in to promote Islam. The Minister for Education is a fervent Muslim and Islam is growing at a staggering rate. Meanwhile, the church is largely apathetic of late, complacently rejoicing about having a Christian President. The group which GLO supports in reaching out to Muslims has, to all intents and purposes, imploded over the last year, and a lengthy reconciliation initiative is struggling to bear fruit. The needs in this area are absolutely urgent. We can't just watch passively from the sidelines as Muslims evangelize so aggressively and effectively. Once converted to Islam, it is very hard to leave again. I deal with a number of former Muslims who have received death threats, have been disowned and kicked out by their families, and have lost their livelihoods. Saying "Jesus is Lord" is a costly decision for them.

Last week the fifth generation of Guillebauds arrived in Burundi. Little Zac is settling in slowly and hopefully adapting to the heat. Yesterday the delighted band at Youth for Christ joined hands in a circle round him to praise the Lord for him and commit his life to God.

Yes, God's story is an exciting one. Here's to you and me being His intimate allies, living recklessly, passionately and dangerously for Him!

Perks without pain?

14 April 2006

Today is Good Friday and Sunday is Easter, but how many of us want Easter perks without Calvary pain? A friend of mine wrote:

> We are more concerned with happiness than holiness. We seek to be served rather than to serve. We want a church that makes us feel good rather than one which challenges us. So often we opt for a religion that costs us little. We stress our rights, not our responsibilities; our freedom in Christ rather than our debt to Christ; our security rather than our sacrifice.

These are challenging words.

I've just returned from an amazing youth rally. SU invited about 300 strategic leaders from schools around the country to come and spend four days together – at a cost of just $3,000, which shows how far money can go out here. The living conditions at the school we hired were basic in the extreme, but amazingly, nobody got seriously sick and we had a wild time. The young people were so spiritually hungry, starting the day at 6.30 a.m. and continuing until 10.30 p.m. For these guys, following Jesus is no picnic.

John had been studying at the very school we were meeting in when the war kicked in. Immediately, students split along tribal lines. He did the same, but felt very uncomfortable with it. After a few days a group of students murdered the headmaster and some teachers from the other tribe. The military surrounded the school and things "settled down" – at least for John, as he was from the "right" tribe, but he left his tribesmen and joined up with four Christians from the other side to pray. Because of this he was repeatedly warned that he would get killed with them, but he stood firm. After three weeks, his fellow tribesmen told him they were coming the following morning to kill him as a traitor. He and the other believers prayed that, just as Daniel was protected when the Lord closed the mouths of the lions, so they would be able to escape unscathed.

The next day they just sauntered past the students and the guards, greeting them nonchalantly, and then ran from the school compound. When the students realized that John and the others had escaped, they chased them through the bush for miles, but didn't catch them. John said that the whole of the following year, when things had calmed down and he had resumed his studies, his life was a nightmare, as people from his own tribe constantly spat in his face because of how he'd behaved. But good on him, I say, following his Leader. Now those people both fear and respect him because he knows what they did, yet he didn't compromise himself.

Another lad, François, shared how after the previous SU camp he had gone back to school so on fire that he preached non-stop in the open air during lunch breaks. Lots of staff and students came to listen to him. People were being converted, so he ended up getting expelled for preaching the gospel. Other students who had converted received written warnings and their parents were summoned to a meeting. François told the others not to worry about him, that he'd be back at school on Monday morning, because God would be faithful.

At the parents' meeting someone asked the headmistress, "So let me get this straight: you have expelled this boy for telling the kids to love and support each other, to respect their superiors, and not to cheat, steal, lie and sleep around. But you have never expelled a student for lying, cheating, stealing or sleeping around?"

The headmistress was cornered. She accepted François back on condition that he agreed to preach only at the school Christian Union meetings!

There were many more great testimonies and I am convinced the effects will be far-reaching. I have returned deeply encouraged, after what have been a tricky few months. Our work is contested at every level because, I believe, it is so strategic.

Recently our outreach to Muslims suffered another massive setback. The woman in charge forged a signature and ran off with all the money – $15,000 in all. It has been a real mess. She's been caught, has admitted her crime, faces a maximum ten years in jail, but has probably bribed the police because they aren't being at all helpful. I long for us to get the money back and for Marie to be truly repentant. It has knocked the stuffing out of me, and has been a bad witness to people watching what is going on. Converts from Islam have such a hard time and are in desperate need of our help. As well as Saleh, another Muslim leader has converted to Christ. The churches are so poor, however, they can't seem to do anything to support these men who will undoubtedly lose their livelihoods, receive death threats, and often have to flee. Mahmoud now lives in a hovel, his wife has just given birth, he has no money, and people want to kill him. But he is still holding firm. The events of Calvary are so very real to these men.

As we celebrate the mystery and wonder of Easter (and I am not talking about how the Easter Bunny manages to lay eggs!), I choose to resist settling for a bland, feel-good, safe and sanitized gospel which bypasses the costly realities of Calvary and is therefore devoid of resurrection power. I choose to live as though Christ died yesterday, rose from the grave today, and is coming back tomorrow – with joy, hope, passion, and urgency, having counted the cost and embraced the challenge to lay down my life for Him. No compromise!

Utter darkness
30 May 2006

Albert van den Heurell wrote: "To pray 'Give us this day our daily bread' and then refuse to share it when the prayer is amply answered is blasphemy!"

I don't fully agree, at least not with the blasphemy part, but he has a point. I've just read an article written about the conflict in the Eastern Congo by Johann Hari. He highlights afresh our complicity as developed nations in the worst conflict since the Second World War:

> It starts with a ward full of women who have been gang-raped and then shot in the vagina... most have wrapped themselves deep in their blankets so I can only see their eyes staring blankly at me. Dr Mukwege is speaking, "Around 10 per cent of them have had this happen to them. We are trying to reconstruct their vaginas, their anuses, their intestines. It is a long process"... Even in this small province, South Kivu, the UN estimates that 45,000 women were raped last year alone. "Crippling their women cripples their society"... The rape of the thousands of women who stagger into the Panzi hospital are, I soon discover, part of a larger rape – the rape of Congo.

This is where you and I come in. Do you have a phone, a laptop, or a games console? To satisfy the West's need for such things, Congo is being perpetually gang-raped to access its precious minerals: coltan, cassiterite, diamonds, etc. I don't want to oversimplify such complex issues, but I do want us to engage and wrestle with them. Ignorance is bliss, but we are not called to choose ignorance, even if it's a more comfortable option which will allow us to continue our current lifestyle with an untroubled conscience. As Oona King, a British politician who was out here recently observed, "Kids in Congo are being sent down mines to die so that kids in Europe and America can kill imaginary aliens in their living rooms." It's a sick world. I sometimes feel totally helpless in the face of such brutal evil, but the least we can do is pray, starting with Frank Laubach's words: "Lord, forgive us for looking at the world with dry eyes."

Yet, it is on this, the "Dark Continent", that often the light indeed shines brightest. I'm continually humbled at the costly experiential reality of Jesus in my brothers' and sisters' lives out here. Many of them literally need to pray, "Give us this day our daily bread" every day, and they share sacrificially out of the little they have when that prayer is answered. I preached in an internally displaced camp a while ago. There were tens of thousands of people in it, many dying day after day. After church I was led into a tin shack and these people, who were starving to death, gave me a plate of rice and beans. What generosity, giving their everything out of their nothing. So often I give just a little out of my plenty.

It's true and it works!
22 August 2006

I'm involved in gospel work because I believe that (1) it's true, and (2) it works. One of the key local leaders we support in Burundi is Onesphore, the founder of a group called Harvest for Christ. He is quite simply the most amazing man of vision, gifting and faith I have come across. He was born in 1972, just two days before the genocide kicked in, so his weak mother had to flee with him on her back. On the sixth day of their fleeing, she wanted to ditch him in the bush, as he was slowing her group down and might be the cause of the whole family being killed, but his father insisted, "No, we will all live or die together." Onesphore says the Lord saved him on that day for a purpose and although he trained as a lawyer, he immediately abandoned his prospects of affluence and a lucrative career when he heard the Lord's call to raise up and equip a new generation of fearless disciples to minister in Burundi and beyond. For the last two weeks he has sent out 140 trained young people without money to ten remote unreached areas to share the Good News with the people they come across. The results have been phenomenal. I'll give you just a sample from his email to me today:

> The young evangelists spoke to about 16,500 people during the two weeks. Approximately 5,500 gave their lives to the Lord, including 20 witch doctors. Six couples about to divorce were reconciled. Three people about to commit suicide were saved. One of them had been cheated on by her husband, so she went to the witch doctor for advice, but he abused her trust by making her pregnant. Just as she was about to kill herself, the young preachers pitched up at her door and led her to Christ!
>
> At twenty different destinations people burned amulets and charms. Two churches were planted. One of those had 650 new converts and a newly built structure which a number of people worked on in a few days, using the proceeds from one man's generous sale of his cow! Twenty-two people were healed, including some demon-possessed people and madmen. In one instance, the locals challenged the visitors, "If you want us to believe you are God's servants, pray for this madman." They prayed for him, went and burned all the charms at his father's house, and he was healed! 212 people were trained up in Evangelism Explosion so as to continue the work by following up on those who had made commitments.

There was plenty of opposition during the week, including a lady reporting one team to the authorities, accusing them of being rebel infiltrators. Consequently, a soldier beat up one of the evangelists, not believing what he was doing. But that same lady who had lied to the authorities subsequently received Christ and repented, then came to seek forgiveness from those she'd slandered. *Yes, the gospel is indeed true and it most definitely works!*

Plain ordinary
23 August 2006

I wrote to GLO's oldest supporter, Alison Hall, the other day, asking her more about herself. She wrote the following today, which is a real challenge to anyone wanting to be used by God. It shows us that we can all get involved and make a real difference:

> As for me... plain ordinary! Dr Stanley-Smith got me interested in the Rwanda Mission in 1936 and we started a prayer meeting, keeping it up till all the others were dead. I drove round to their houses to pick them up for it. I still survive at ninety-six years old and pray on. It is a great privilege and joy, and you keep me well up with prayer fuel. We have a little country market where I can sell things I make. So for forty years, I baked madly. Now I just make meringues when I can and knit soft toys which bring in a bit. Perhaps Rwanda and Burundi will be written on my heart! God has been so good to me all my life that I can't do enough for Him.

Like Alison, I'm very ordinary. But God is extraordinary. He can take us ordinary duffers and do extraordinary things through us – but the deal is complete surrender. Are we willing to "consider everything a loss compared to the surpassing greatness of knowing Christ Jesus [as] Lord" (Philippians 3:8)? Or did He die on the cross for us to settle for a blunt, dull, self-absorbed, middle-class consumer religion?

No, there's so much more. Let's abandon our own feeble stories and play our part in God's Great Story.

15

A REORDERING OF PRIORITIES

Life is a war. That is not all it is, but it is always that.

John Piper

Loving headbutts
20 October 2006

I want to contrast these two different pictures of life in Burundi:

1. A few weeks ago, some people spotted the bloody body of a prisoner floating in the river. When they investigated further, they found a number of bodies skewered on a long branch like a kebab. The reports were initially completely denied, but human rights groups went and took photos of the bodies, verifying the gruesome claims. It turns out that twenty-six prisoners had been taken out and murdered in this brutal fashion. Only because the press has made a big deal of this has it come to public knowledge.

2. Little Zac is ten months old and growing fast. At this stage he is totally unaware of the evil and brutality that surrounds him in this world. For him it's a nice enough place. Since last week he has started to consciously wave goodbye to people. His latest development, which has brought such joy to Lizzie and me, is when I say to him, "Zac, give me a kiss!" and he lurches forward clumsily and headbutts me on the lips! This morning he joined me in worshiping the Lord with my guitar. He's definitely a budding charismatic, waving both hands in the air, accompanied by ecstatic squeals!

You can see how I struggle to reconcile the world where people are skewered on a branch like a kebab with the world of Zac's loving headbutts. Yet, that sums up life in Burundi. Extra-judicial killings have been commonplace and respect for the rule of law seems non-existent. Even the judges have gone on strike in protest at the current situation. These are crucial times – still. Apparently peace has come, now that the last rebel group has signed up to the ceasefire. But in actual fact, it's almost worse now. As a friend said to me, "People were getting killed before, but that's normal in wartime. It shouldn't happen if there is peace."

More disturbing than that is the privileged position being given to Islam. The country is receiving a great deal of funding from Islamic regimes who expect something in return. The *quid pro quo* is the active (and not very subtle) promotion of Muslims to key positions of influence where they can accelerate the transformation of society in their direction. I have just spoken to a high-profile Muslim convert to Christ who has received death threats, has been terrorized at his home, and who has gone from riches to rags following his conversion from Islam. Islam means "submission". Those who say it is a religion of peace are partly right – if you are willing to submit. If you are not, then peace is the last word that comes to mind. Our work with converts from Islam to

Christ (apostates) reveals nothing but suffering and pain, with them routinely getting kicked out of their families, losing their jobs, being totally ostracized and facing the very real possibility of being killed.

These precious brothers and sisters challenge me on how much I am willing to sacrifice for Jesus. Am I prepared to lose everything for Him? I often come back to the question of whether I am following Jesus or whether He is following me on my terms. My life is ridiculously easy compared to these people. What does it cost me to follow Jesus? To worship with those who have submitted to the crucible of sharing in Christ's sufferings is a humbling experience.

Back to Zac and me, worshipping God together on the guitar. This morning it made me think of the Greek word for worship – *proskyneo* – which means, literally, "to lean forward and kiss". Such is the intimacy our Heavenly Father desires with us. I'll be honest and admit that there are times, plenty of them, when I look at the problems of Burundi and get totally discouraged, almost sinking in despair. I've felt like that in the last few weeks. I can talk a good game most of the time, but it hurts to deliver the goods. We get wounded, bruised, tired, disillusioned, broken and discouraged. Intimacy with God? I want to be in that place, but it's frequently elusive, and in any case, feelings are often deceptive. The best proof of our love for God is our obedience to Him. "Whoever has my commands and obeys them, he is the one who loves me. He who loves me will be loved by my Father, and I too will love him and show myself to him" (John 14:21).

I have His commands, but am I obeying them? Do I love people extravagantly, make time for what (more often "who") really matters, share my faith, give sacrificially to God's work, step out of my comfort zone? If we are living out the gospel, it has to hit us and hurt us somewhere. I fear we're often a disobedient bunch.

Yet, the promise is so vast and our understanding so limited. Surely I'll give my all if I really grasp the truth of Jesus' words: "He who loves me will be loved by my Father, and *I too will love him and show myself to him.*" That's where the intimacy lies.

I know that I am sometimes lazy and disobedient and I need a kick up the backside. Other times, I know I gave it my best shot. Even if it wasn't great, I obeyed. When Zac leans forward and headbutts me on the lips, I respond by kissing, cuddling and squeezing him closely. The love I feel is quite overwhelming. I sense my Heavenly Father receiving my worship in the same way, even if my best efforts resemble a clumsy, badly aimed headbutt!

Father God, help me to be an obedient worshipper in Spirit and in truth, that my sacrifice of praise may be acceptable to you!

Marriage messiness
29 November 2006

During this period Lizzie and I struggled in our marriage, so I wrote to my "inner circle" of accountability partners to get their thoughts:

Lizzie has encouraged me to write to you, as we're struggling right now.

Life is great. I feel so blessed. I don't know why things seem to go so well for me. Generally, whatever I get involved in seems to work. Now, at the end of 2006, I find myself living in Burundi with a fabulous wife, a gorgeous healthy son, a very stimulating and stretching job, heading up a growing and exciting organization, and there are simply so many positives.

But, on the other hand, life is not great. In the last few months, on a different level, I have become progressively more and more discouraged and absorbed in the problems of Burundi. It probably started as soon as we returned here in late September. We'd just had a great summer with lots of fun with family and friends. We raced around the UK, preaching, selling books, enjoying precious times, and it was very energizing. Then – *bang!* – we were back in Burundi. Whereas the end of 2005 was so wonderfully encouraging for Burundi and its people, now the outlook is bleak once again. The initial honeymoon period of peaceful transition to democratic rule has given way to a climate of restricted freedom of speech, gross human rights violations, an emasculated judiciary, the sidelining (read "imprisoning") of political opponents, and the privileging of Islam in an extraordinary way.

It is the last of these problems that has brought me down the most. It is staggering. I doubt there is another place on Earth where a nation is being transformed so fast. The Christian President has his hands tied financially and so is restricted by the Muslim Party Chairman, who is clearly and widely acknowledged as the most powerful man in the land. He literally does what he wants. The former Vice-President consequently resigned, citing the Chairman's unreasonable and incessant intervention in governmental affairs, before fleeing the country. She was a Christian and was replaced by the Chairman's cousin, another Muslim of course, with dubious claims to Burundian citizenship.

The church is quiet on all this. Brave enough journalists are now either fleeing the country or are incarcerated in prison. So many young people are turning to Islam, and they are the future of the nation. I am watching this, trying to motivate the church leaders (I am writing this during a seminar on Islam I have pushed for, and it is blowing them all away), screaming inside and getting depressed as a result.

The problem is, I can't seem to do my bit and leave the rest to God! It sounds ridiculous, but I think "big picture" the whole time and take all Burundi's problems on my shoulders. I just can't let go. It means I am withdrawn more and more and Lizzie has noticed it. I should be able to switch off and enjoy our family time, but it is always there, weighing me down.

This has, of course, affected our marriage. How Lizzie and I describe the state of our marriage is instructive of how we see life. I've always said we have a *great* marriage. She has always said we have a *good* marriage. I tend to see things in brighter or more extreme shades. At the moment I describe our marriage as "OK". Lizzie says that it's "not great". I am sure the issue is how heavily weighed down I feel.

Consequently, our communication is being hindered. Quality time is Lizzie's love language (i.e. her emotional needs are met through my spending real quality time with her). But when she wants to talk, I'm too caught up with my own thoughts and my head feels as though it will explode with anger at the injustice here – the guilt about how much we have, the sense of helplessness I feel at Islam's progress and the discouragement of the country going down the tubes after such an amazing turnaround. Lizzie is rightly consumed with baby talk, while I'm at the other end of the spectrum, wanting to save the universe.

Whenever we are back in the UK, I still feel these issues keenly, of course, but they are thousands of miles away, so I'm better able to switch off and enjoy life, compartmentalizing things more effectively. But here, from listening to the call to prayer at 4.30 a.m., opening the gates and driving past beggars, receiving umpteen requests for anything and everything, to hearing so many sob stories, I sometimes feel like I am going to crack up. But, hear this: I don't want sympathy. Getting sympathy will only make me feel more guilty, because my lot is a piece of cake next to 99.98 per cent (at a guess) of the population of this desperate country. How dare I moan, groan and complain? But that's how I feel.

One other issue, I think, is that I don't feel challenged in the same way as previous years. I am a pioneer by nature and this is a season of consolidation. I need to keep stretching myself and pushing barriers or I feel bored and unfulfilled. Maybe that's just tough luck for me right now and I need to knuckle down? It certainly adds to my internal malaise.

So, Agony Uncles, any words of wisdom? I am not depressed, but my mind is clearly in an unhealthy state. Whatever stage of "badness" things have got to, I want to acknowledge where I am at and rectify the situation. I'm asking for your help, if you have anything to offer me!

Truth in love
5 December 2006

I love my accountability partners, all seven of them. They each fed back to me plenty of insights and have been a huge support in speaking the truth to me in love. Here are a couple of the guys' comments, which I need to listen to carefully:

> Your email is troublesome reading and I'm glad you're reaching out to us. That Lizzie is a good woman!
>
> The issues with which you're grappling are truly burdensome, and in some way I think are part of carrying the cross: feeling the pains of Burundi, the onslaught of evil there, the disunity of the church. I do think that's part of the life of a Christian – to carry the burdens of others and feel the agony that the Lord feels. With you seeing such things face to face, it would be odd for you not to feel it deeply in your heart. So my first thought is to praise the Lord that he has given you such a heart of compassion and love for the people of Burundi, and such a deep burden for the growth of His kingdom and the unity of His people. These are all good

and right, even if heavy, heavy, things to feel as a child of God, as described to us in the Scriptures. This is the way of the cross.

But something isn't quite right in how you're carrying your burden. The freedom and joy we have from being in Christ is in knowing that *He* is the Lord and that the final victory over sin and death (our own and the world's) is assured. The way you describe your reaction to current events, as understandable as they are, demonstrates confidence neither in Christ's Lordship, nor in His final victory. You say you can't let go, you can't do your bit and entrust the rest to God. Why not? Do you think what you're holding onto is actually changing anything, improving things? In fact, given that this is eating away at your ability to love Lizzie and Zac, isn't your holding on to these things doing precisely the opposite of what you intend? It's the height of tragic irony if, in your zeal and burden to see the gospel of grace and love grow in Burundi, it diminishes in your own relationships.

This is what happens when we act like Jesus isn't the Lord, like He isn't quite doing enough, like if *we* don't do something Satan will ultimately win. I hate to put this so harshly, Simon, but it's imperative that you embody what you want for Burundi in your relationship with Lizzie and Zac. Trusting in the Lord and believing in His final victory means, in your life right now, that you are *obedient* to Him in His calling on your life; nothing more, nothing less. He is going to save Burundi by His sovereign power and by each member of His body doing what he/she is called to do. This, I think, is where you need to direct your prayer to the Lord, to know that you are doing His will. The question is not "am I doing enough?", but "am I doing His will?"… "am I being obedient to Him?"

The answer to that question about obedience should also help you with the guilty feelings regarding your apparent well-being. Virtue doesn't come from feeling bad that you have more than others, and it doesn't come from voluntary poverty; it comes from being grateful that all good things come from the hand of the Lord. I don't know this, but I'm tempted to think that those who are poorer than you would despise you if they knew you were sitting there wracked with guilt because of your "wealth". "Hey, if you're feeling so bad about it, stop complaining and just give it to me!" I share the same problem in feeling permanently guilty about my good fortune, but seriously, all you're doing is feeling guilty about it but doing nothing to change it. That's worldly sorrow and it brings death. So, either be glad and grateful for what you have, or if you think this guilt is from the Holy Spirit, take yourself and your family, hand over all your possessions and live how and where you think He wants you to live (all this is nicely summed up in 2 Corinthians 7:10 and Philippians 4:12).

Finally, in *The Great Divorce* by C. S. Lewis, there's a section that impressed me deeply. I think it goes like this (and the point here isn't you and Lizzie, but about gospel joy and the presence of evil and suffering): a wife is in such a place of utter delight and joy in "Heaven" that she cannot contain it. She meets her unbelieving husband who is in chains and is dull and grey and miserable. He's perplexed that she won't stop smiling even as she looks upon him with pity. But she can't stop her joy, and won't. The point being that if she did, then ultimately evil, death, hell, suffering, tears and weeping wins and there is no hope. If we Christians do not carry love and joy and the fullness of life in us in the midst of suffering and evil, then the evil wins, and hope is crushed. Somehow, even through the burdens and suffering you endure for the sake of Burundi in the name of Jesus Christ, you need to hold on firmly to the joy set before you (Hebrews 12), and the love poured out into your heart by the Holy Spirit (Romans 5). That is your victory even now, Simon, and is going to be the thing that enables God's work to flourish *in* you even as He works through you.

Another brother wrote:

> I have thought long and hard before replying to this. Who am I to give advice in this matter? I believe I am the world's worst at all the issues you have raised. I feel such a hypocrite to even start this email, but I do so because I love you guys and to remain silent would be criminal at a time like this. I may actually be convicted of what I am writing myself and get my finger out! There is also the fact that having been there and been hurt, I do know what you are talking about, and I do know why it all turned to worms for me, and I do know that if I had done things differently I would be in a better place now.
>
> So here goes... some lessons learnt, bitterly:
>
> 1. God does not need you to sort out the problems in Burundi. He can do it quite well without you. He has chosen to use you there because He wants to bless you. If for whatever reason you need some time out, God has plenty of other people lined up. You will never be indispensable to His plan for Burundi.
>
> 2. You may not consider yourself depressed, but no one ever does at the outset, especially men. If you were to run down a stress checklist you would find you have a very high score, so you need to take action *before* you *feel* depressed.
>
> 3. Men operate on a completely different planet from women.
>
> 4. Lizzie just needs you to be there for her, not to have lots of clever answers or promises. Men always want to give an answer. But being there in person, when your mind is on one hundred and one other things is not what she needs. While you are in the centre of all the action, with all the drop-in visitors and interruptions, your mind will never be totally given over to the girl you love. You need to get away together, just for a short break. And then do it again. And again. One quick fix will not work.

5. Satan hates you being there. He has seen the effect you have had and he will do anything to ruin your (God's) work. The quickest way he could destroy your ministry is through an attack on your relationship with Lizzie. I was aware of this all the time we were in Sumatra and made sure we had our armor on every day, without fail. I did not expect it at Allnations. I probably did not feel my presence there was strategically vital, so I got blasé about the spiritual attacks. When it hit, it was a broadside that sent me reeling. I survived, badly scarred, and I lived to fight another day. But Lara and I both realize how close we came to disaster, and we never saw it coming.

I am going to stop there, my keyboard is in danger of being swamped with tears.

One of the very practical decisions I have taken is to stop working from home, because that creates a much clearer separation between work and family time. Before, I would always be nipping off to answer another few emails, so Lizzie would never feel that I was truly "there". She was right, my mind was constantly focused on other things. The impact and improvement has been immediate, which is very encouraging. I thank God for Lizzie, for our marriage, and also for key friends who encourage us. By God's grace I'll improve as a husband and father.

16

A Horizon of Hope

In our day Heaven and Earth are on tiptoe waiting for the
emergence of a Spirit-led, Spirit-intoxicated, Spirit-empowered
people.

Richard Foster

Seismic changes
8 February 2007

The last six weeks have seen some of the most seismic changes
in Burundi's recent history. It could not have been more
(positively) tense, dramatic and exciting. The whole country
has been gripped, tuning into various radio stations almost
by the hour to see whether this nascent democracy would
pull through or crumble in the face of a ruthless and corrupt
Party Chairman, whose Machiavellian behavior showed utter
contempt for the rule of law. So what has happened? I'll sum
it up as briefly as possible:

At the turn of the year, the overtly Christian President
sponsored a huge evangelistic outreach at the national
stadium. It was a powerful time, at which he promised that

the year 2007 would bring big changes. Within a few days, two wrongfully arrested journalists, and then six alleged coup-plotters were released, undermining the autocratic (Muslim) Party Chairman, who (it is widely accepted) had ordered them to be locked up.

As I mentioned in the previous chapter, the Party Chairman (PC) was the *de facto* leader of the country, doing almost whatever he wanted. Human rights abuses were common, and journalists were being bumped off or forced to flee the country – all traceable back to the PC. From a Christian perspective, it was disastrous, as Islam was gaining ground at a staggering rate with all the PC's cohorts promoted into positions of power, privileging their own with opportunities such as building mosques and Islamic schools and plundering the nation's coffers to line their own pockets. In his arrogance the PC openly threatened the press and any possible opposition was ruthlessly quashed. Hence the alleged attempted *coup d'état*, which saw the former President and Vice-President locked up without any proof for six months (it was most likely a set-up to marginalize potentially powerful opponents), as well as two journalists for the "crime" of questioning the veracity of the coup claims.

I was so discouraged and downbeat at the turn of the year, and it definitely took its toll on Lizzie and me. As petro-dollars were being pumped in from the Middle East to help the expansion of Islam, the situation looked so grim. But the body of Christ was praying, fasting and crying out to God! I won't overplay our role, but I and a few others undertook an initiative behind the scenes which has to remain secret, to protect some key people. Suddenly there was a complete turnaround and people had had enough. The President started addressing the issues. He stood up to the PC who had helped him into power in the first place. Then yesterday, praise the Lord, the PC was booted out, ending a terrible sixteen-month post-election rule of terror and abuse. The PC has declared the meeting illegal and the battle rages on, but most nationals are rejoicing. There were people jumping with joy and the newly appointed replacement PC duly committed himself to implementing changes for the betterment of Burundi according to the constitution, and – wait for it – the Bible!

Burundi is truly a crazy place! Life is never dull. I love this country.

I am so proud to see how Burundi's democratic institutions have just about managed to pull through this massive test. The press had a huge role to play in it. There are still significant issues to be addressed: the President has plenty of enemies and the former PC is very powerful. The battle continues...

None of this made the world's headlines last night because little Burundi doesn't have oil like Iraq, but yesterday as a mini-Saddam was booted out peacefully (so far), it was an historic turning-point in the emergence of this tiny nation. I am not being triumphalistic, because that would be naïve and premature. We still have a very long way to go. In fact, the University of Leicester's School of Psychology did a study on the levels of happiness of all countries in the world, and its findings have just been released. Burundi came bottom!

Casting the vision
19 March 2007

It is nine years ago now that I heard God's call to go to Burundi, left family, friends, my job and my security, and landed in a crazy war zone. It was so dangerous that I honestly expected my days would soon be over. Plenty of others died around me, but my time obviously wasn't up and the Lord still had work for me to do.

Those early days were amazing. I arrived with very little money, most of which soon got stolen anyway, borrowed a bicycle off an older missionary and started evangelizing as part of the SU team. SU was bankrupt and unable to do much, but the vision was there. A new chapter had begun. God's grace and favor were on our work and the growth and impact were amazing. We opened up two regional offices and two new departments (children's ministry and "Aid for AIDS"). From using a bike to a motorbike to a 4x4 truck, I was preaching around the country like a headless chicken, risking my life on ambush-prone roads in rebel-controlled territory. It wasn't easy. But the rawness and desperation of the situation fuelled my passion to give everything to see people come to Christ before they died. Maybe that sounds melodramatic – but the fact is, life was truly dramatic.

The longer I stayed here, the more I realized that my potential contribution to the church in Burundi could be multiplied and leveraged by identifying the most gifted Burundian believers and empowering them to transform their own nation for Christ. They could do the job better than me – after all, it was their country, their language and their culture. By this time people were giving me so much money that we were legally required to set up a charity.

This is how Great Lakes Outreach was born. As well as funding the growing activities of SU, we helped Evangelism Explosion take off nationally, were part of the start-up of a group reaching out to Muslims, provided seed-funding to help launch and consolidate Youth for Christ, Harvest for Christ, a ministry reaching out to the universities, an orphanage, and a street kids project. I can only say that the people running these ministries are of the highest integrity, vision and passion for Christ. I learn so much from them. They humble me. It is a privilege to get alongside them and help them be released and unleashed to accomplish their dreams in Jesus' name. Between us, we are being used to do some amazing things. A friend who was working here in 2000 came back to visit a few weeks ago and said how incredible it was to see what the Lord was doing through us since those humble beginnings. To God alone be the glory!

Now, praise God, the seemingly impossible has happened. Peace has come and the country is rebuilding. The opportunities are remarkable. There are huge problems to address, but we are moving in the right direction and God's people are playing a massive role in this nation.

Now consider this statement: "A missionary's job is to do himself out of a job."

I wonder whether you agree? The fact is, that is what I am aiming for. My biggest attempt in that direction is the building of a conference center to generate funds that will then be pumped back into evangelism and discipleship programs throughout the country. We are progressing very well with it and the skeletons of the three big buildings (300-seater and 100-seater conference rooms, an administrative block with a restaurant, a sports gym, and a 30-bedroom guest house) are nearly complete. It will be the best conference center in the country, we hope. This is the vision I have for it:

The vision is not bricks and mortar, it's about transforming the nation. It's about investing in the next generation. It's about developing leaders. It's about providing the church with a resource for them to use. It's about creating self-sustainability which will enable SU to be guaranteed a steady source of income for countrywide evangelism for years to come. It's about empowering local believers in a dirt-poor country to stand on their own two feet. It's about lifting the name of Jesus over the nation of Burundi. It's about providing excellence in His name. And by faith, it'll be a reality within a couple of years. Watch this space!

It can happen again
20 April 2007

I just read the following:

> In our day Heaven and Earth are on tiptoe waiting for the
> emergence of a Spirit-led, Spirit-intoxicated, Spirit-empowered
> people. All of creation watches expectantly for the springing up
> of a disciplined, freely-gathered, martyr people who know in this
> life the life and power of the kingdom of God. It has happened
> before. It can happen again...
>
> **Richard Foster**

What are we waiting for? It can happen again.

Last week, a group from Cheltenham joined the SU team
up-country for part of a youth camp. Numbers had been
limited to 300, but in the end 450 came, saying that we couldn't
keep them away – they were prepared to sleep outside under
the stars if necessary! There were eight youths sharing each
double mattress. The conditions, as always, were very basic,
but the students' thirst was insatiable and the Lord moved
in powerful ways. Over the four days many repented and
most who had arrived unconverted left with a vibrant new-
found faith to take back to the dozens of schools represented.
Investing in the youth is so very strategic.

From there we drove another hour towards the Tanzanian
border to visit the New Generation street kids project we
support. It was shattering to hear from one of my best friends,
Joe, on our arrival that his three-year-old daughter had been
raped by one of the older street kids whom Joe had rescued
from the streets and looked after for the last ten years. I wept
in anger, disgust and sadness. Little Sarai is undergoing
treatment to minimize the risk of HIV infection. What
amazed me, though, was how Joe was clinging to the Lord

and at peace. He was gutted, obviously, but acknowledging that the enemy will try anything to undermine and destroy the ministry. Yet nothing would stop the work of God that they were doing.

Today I saw my colleague, Clara, for the first time in a while. She'd been visiting her brother in Rwanda. I asked her how it had gone and she replied, "Terribly." I asked why and she told me, "I had to have him arrested for raping a young girl." Such events leave me with so many questions: Why? How? There are a lot of sick people around. Rape has become a tool of war all over this region.

I often find visitors from the West manage to see things and express them very clearly when they are confronted with the rawness of life out here and observe how people live out a costly faith. Here is what a few of them have written to me recently:

It's so hard to get people to understand the big picture back here in the USA, but that doesn't slow me down. I preached on 1 Peter 1:22; 2:3, the perishable versus the imperishable. Everyone's typical response is that we have to "find a balance", but I just don't find Jesus teaching or living that principle – it kind of seemed all or nothing to me. Everyone's just so afraid of what it would mean to live radically for Him.

It was funny arriving home – the reverse culture shock was really quite something. I felt like we saw Western culture for what it really is: fairly disgusting, to be honest! The consumerist, individualistic, short-termist, desire for pain-free-living culture that we live in as Brits is quite contrary to the gospel. I'm challenged about how we put ourselves at the centre of our world. We start asking God to be part of our story rather than keeping the focus on our being part of His story.

It's amazing, but obvious, really, just how much God can do with fully surrendered lives. In Burundi we met a number of them – people doing incredible things, against incredible odds, because they held nothing back. Do I love Jesus enough to surrender to that level?

Do I? I want to. What's it worth? It can happen again... Let's do it!

What is the gospel?
1 May 2007

I'm back in the UK for a visit and I've just been to one of the biggest churches in the country and listened to what I gather is their regular weekly fare in the one-hour sermon. It sounds so crass, you can't believe people can possibly be taken in, but they are, by their thousands. Essentially the message goes like this:

> Come to Jesus and He'll take away your problems. He's got a wonderful plan for your life. He wants to bless you and make you happy. He promises fullness of life, but maybe you've been looking for that fullness in the wrong places, be it through sex or your career or money. They won't satisfy. Come to Jesus and receive all the blessings He wants to pour into your life. He'll make you rich. Just claim His promises and have faith that they will come to pass.

On and on it goes along the same theme. It makes me positively angry. It's such a twisting of the truth. I mean, how would that message sound to believers in North Korea today, or in Saudi Arabia or Iraq? Following Christ for many of them involves imprisonment, torture, losing their jobs, death threats and expulsion from their families. "Hey, come to Jesus, He'll take away your problems and make you happy!" Give me a break!

Then, almost in the same breath, when the appeal is made for people to come forward to receive that wonderful plan for their lives, the preacher lists all those who are sick and dying, depressed and lonely, grieving and hurting, but nobody seems to see the disconnect. As Ray Comfort and Kurt Cameron comment in *The Way of the Master*:

> He promises a bed of roses for those who come to Christ, but for those who are already in Christ, they are experiencing a painful bed of thorns. He promises a smooth flight, but for those who are already on board, they are experiencing extreme turbulence.

These myriad preachers, who preach what itching ears want to hear, totally ignore so many key scriptures. So what is the gospel? How about Jesus' words in John 16:33: "In this world you will have trouble." *Ouch!* "But take heart! I have overcome the world." *Oof!*

That's the gospel in a nutshell. We embrace both parts. The cross we bear precedes the crown we wear. People want all blessing and no cost, which is a twisted, man-centered gospel and leads to people falling away at an alarming rate when things get tough, because they'd been told everything would be easy once they gave their life to Jesus. What a lie! May I be faithful in preaching an authentic message of beautiful, costly discipleship.

I don't have a theology of grim, morbid suffering for Christ, but neither do I ignore verses like 2 Timothy 3:12: "In fact, everyone who wants to live a godly life in Christ Jesus will be persecuted."

I've just read this in Dietrich Bonhoeffer's book, *The Cost of Discipleship*, written in prison shortly before he was executed by the Nazis:

Suffering is the badge of true discipleship. The disciple is not above his master... That is why Luther reckoned suffering among the marks of the true church... if we refuse to take up our cross and submit to suffering and rejection at the hands of men, we forfeit our fellowship with Christ and have ceased to follow Him. But if we lose our lives in His service and carry our cross, we shall find our lives again in the fellowship of the cross with Christ.

Let's not opt for a comfortable, easy Christianity (which in truth does not exist), but instead let's determine to "lose our lives in His service".

17

THE ART OF PERSEVERANCE

Obstacles are those frightful things you see when you take your eyes off the goal.

John Isaacs

Eyes on the goal
28 May 2007

It's so very easy to take my eyes off the goal. So many things compete for my attention. I'm bombarded with apparently urgent tasks which need doing. I've found myself almost overwhelmed recently with the number of "plates" I seem to be juggling, concerned that one or more will go crashing to pieces when my guard is down. Well, the good news is that they are all still in the air at the moment, and I don't doubt it's because of the massive worldwide prayer backing we receive.

This last weekend's outreach got my eyes firmly back on the goal. I drove our SU team on terrible roads into the bush with a number of volunteers and dropped each one off at a different school with sixty Bibles. The subsidized price for a Bible is just over $4, but that is still far too much for most people (hard to believe, maybe). The system we introduced was that any member of the Christian Union could have a Bible, and they could pay by installments for however long it took. The money collected would then be used to buy more Bibles, so that each school had a constant supply and nobody could have the excuse of not having one. There were whoops of delight wherever we went and many students were touched by the Lord.

At one school, they described what they were going through as "living in the times of the Spirit". There were 230 students in their CU and they had a choir of 40 new converts from this academic year alone. The pastors said that their biggest problem in these times of revival was following up so many students.

I was with my SU colleague, Leonidas, who as a Hutu had to flee from university back in 1996. Students from the other tribe had thrown a grenade into his room as he was praying and he narrowly escaped with his life, needing several operations to remove shrapnel from his eye. He has no bitterness towards his aggressors and often includes the incident as part of his testimony of grace. He was forced to go and live in the bush and used to walk eighteen miles each day to teach at a distant school. The believers met each week on his only day off, so even then he walked all that way, through mud, rain, sunshine, whatever, and all these years on, the fruit is obvious as the whole area seems to be experiencing extraordinary times. God is faithful. Leonidas' eyes, damaged but still shining, are kept firmly on the goal: to change the nation through the powerful message of the risen Christ.

After visits to six separate schools on Saturday we convened twenty schools together on Sunday. I don't think

I've ever experienced another Pentecost Sunday in my life where the people assembled have so clearly undergone their own Pentecost! There were nearly a thousand of us packed into the school refectory. The singing was deafening.

A deacon called Mary was worshipping a few yards away from me. When she was fifteen years old she suddenly went blind, dumb and curled up into a ball, totally paralyzed. For the next six years she only moved if her family picked her up and changed her position. She barely ate a thing. Then some young people came and prayed for her and her sight returned. They persevered in prayer and fasting, and her arms began to move. Finally, her paralysis left her completely but she was still unable to speak. Surely God would grant her full healing? She joined the church choir as a non-singing member(!) and months later, after an evangelistic outing, her mouth opened suddenly and she screamed "Jesus!" She will soon be an ordained pastor. Her testimony has been heard on the radio and has impacted many lives.

Yes, God's Spirit is doing great things in Burundi. The obstacles are huge, the challenges are constant, but He is faithful.

So if obstacles are those things I see when I take my eyes off the goal, I need to ask myself: *What is my goal?*

And, irrespective of any obstacles, *Who or what are my eyes focused on?*

Hebrews 12:2 says: "Let us fix our eyes on Jesus, the author and perfecter of our faith, who for the joy [goal] set before him endured the cross, scorning its shame, and sat down at the right hand of throne of God. Consider him..."

Here's to changing the world as wide-eyed, passionate disciples sacrificing everything for the cause with a clear sight on the goal.

WWJD or WDJD?
30 August 2007

"What Would Jesus Do?" can be a good question in some situations, but it can also be a cop-out at times when we plainly see from the Bible what Jesus did, what His disciples did, and what He expects us in turn to do. J. B. Philips commented after months of in-depth study and translation of the book of Acts:

> These disciples didn't make acts of faith, they believed; they didn't say their prayers, they really prayed; they didn't hold conferences on psychosomatic medicine, they simply healed the sick… The Spirit of God found what He must always be seeking – a fellowship of men and women so united in love and faith that He can work in and through them with the minimum of hindrance.

The Spirit of God is still seeking the same thing.

The last two weeks in Burundi have witnessed such a group of men and women. I've just received a report about what the twenty-three groups of Harvest for Christ evangelists got up to. Ten in each team, they went to fourteen unreached areas and had a massive impact. I know that some reports on evangelism can exaggerate their numbers, but I assure you, these guys are the real deal. I'll translate Onesphore's summary:

> From our door-to-door visiting and outreach, 15,890 people believed and prayed to receive Christ, including 47 witch doctors and 16 Muslims. We burnt talismans and objects of witchcraft in 49 families. There were 45 miraculous healings, including 4 mentally ill and 11 demon-possessed people. 8 couples on the verge of divorce repented and want to make their marriages work. 2 people about

to commit suicide were talked out of it. 308 people were trained for follow-up in different churches.

He goes on:

A famous witch doctor at Ijenda, Joselyne, gave her life to Christ. Her sister refused to believe, but brought over a demon-possessed neighbor. The latter hadn't eaten for three days and Joselyne's sister challenged the believers: "If you heal this girl, I'll know that you are serving the one true God." God duly healed the girl and 21 people (including the sister) promptly gave their lives to Christ. Elsewhere, a group of evangelists were arrested and taken to prison. One lad, whilst in his cell, led two people to Christ! Another team were beaten up, but continued preaching.

That's just a sample.

What would Jesus do today? The same as He did when He was on earth. What should we do today? Surely the same as His followers did then! I know most of us want to be used by God and to see His power at work through us, but how much do we *really* want it? What is it worth to us? What is stopping us or holding us back? There was for the early followers, and will be for us, a cost to this. God wants nothing less than full surrender.

This is my personal challenge today and it hits me hard.

"What Did Jesus Do?" is straightforward enough to verify. My concern with "WWJD" is that it has the inherent flaw of opening the door to speculation. It might allow me to justify, by conjecture, a more moderate and tame response to the wild and dangerous call to follow the costly way of the cross.

Crushed and elated
26 October 2007

Today I feel both crushed and elated. There is so much bad stuff going on, but also some incredibly good stuff. Life is so raw out here, so black and white, such a rollercoaster of highs and lows. It would be so much easier to remain aloof and keep an emotional distance from my adoptive people, but I want to care and I choose to care, although it hurts to care.

I sit listening to friends pouring out their hearts. Burundian men don't cry. As the local proverb puts it, "A Burundian man's tears flow inside his belly." But John does shed some tears as he, aged thirty, shares how his pregnant wife Sarah has recently mysteriously died, leaving young David confused at home and Daddy absolutely devastated. Peter and Ruth have had their fourth and very late miscarriage and are clinging to God to get through the anguish. Alfred comes in and tells me two members of his family have died in my absence. Privat shows up to work after a sleepless night listening to renewed bombing, with the radio reporting eleven dead as factions of the last remaining rebel group kill each other. Joe shares how the street kids' project simply doesn't have money for them to eat, whilst his three-year-old Sarai is recovering from being raped. Unemployed Ildephonse looks at me imploringly and talks of his wife and four kids who have nothing and he can't provide for them.

Meanwhile, corruption scandals are being reported with monotonous regularity. Crime is absolutely rampant. The schools and public universities have been on strike country-wide because salaries aren't being paid. Extremist Muslims are rapidly gaining ground and maximizing the discontent with fiery rhetoric and aggressive evangelism. "In ten years this country will be dominated by Islam," they brazenly claim in their open-air meetings, totally confident and unabashed, riding the wave of massive outside funding.

People are thin, really thin. I get called fat here – can you believe it? It's a compliment, by the way. I'm a skinny runt by any objective standard, but I'm considered fat and well fed here. Most people struggle to afford to eat. The price of some essential foodstuffs has doubled in the last few months. What would I do if I couldn't feed Zac and Lizzie? I think I'd steal too or maybe change religion if the Muslims were offering me some money to help start a little business. Yes, that's what's happening in many instances.

Enough of the depressing stuff, although it needs acknowledging. Yes, there's plenty to get angry, dejected, discouraged and crushed about, but that is only half the story.

Seeing kids at our Youth For Christ orphanage who would otherwise be dead is overwhelming. Little Tom, who was found in a gutter, is at last able to smile for the first time in his two-year-old traumatized life. Six-year-old Helene is, almost unbelievably, no bigger than our two-year-old Zac, but is steadily growing emotionally, physically and spiritually. The school has started and for me to see twenty little lives being frogmarched into their classrooms in their smart uniforms is a joy.

Our outreaches country-wide with SU and Harvest for Christ are amazing. Eleven former witch doctors are now in baptismal classes following the summer evangelistic campaign. Many youths around the country are on fire, leaving their homes to go and share with the lost. I was preaching last Saturday as part of a week-long outreach. The responses are invariably huge. The night before, a cripple had thrown away his crutches in front of everybody, blowing away the Muslims particularly, as they can't really answer or explain away the power of the name of Jesus.

Onesphore sent me another report:

In Gisoro, a madman terrorized a whole village, wandering around for years with a machete. A team came and prayed for him, he was healed, and for the rest of the two weeks' outreach he went around with them testifying to the power of God at work in their lives.

Another team found a girl who hadn't been able to walk for six months. The mother wouldn't let them preach, saying she'd only listen if she saw the power of God healing her daughter. They prayed and told her to get up. She literally hadn't been upright for six months, but she stood. They prayed further and her trembling legs became strong. She walked to church the next day to praise God for her miracle, along with all those who were converted watching the miracle take place.

Another team went straight into a witch doctor's den and started dismantling all his fetishes. He came in and screamed in anger at them. What they were doing was unthinkable. Most people would expect to drop dead if they did such a thing. But these guys knew their power was stronger than the witch doctor's satanic power. There was one particular powder over the entrance that he would use to cause lightning bolts to strike people dead, and he screamed in fear when one lad was about to grab it. "Don't do it or we'll all die!" The lad continued clearing it away and when nothing happened, the witch doctor agreed to burn all his fetishes and give his life to Christ.

I hesitate to tell people in the West these stories, as they may struggle to believe me, but the fact that the witch doctor was so scared himself, having used the powder to kill so many people, shows those more skeptical that at the very least he thought it was real.

The arrival of No. 2
14 November 2007

Grace Tiggy Guillebaud rocked our world as she made her dramatic entrance last night in Southampton General Hospital at 11.44 p.m., weighing in at 8lb 4oz, looking very blue for a while, but in perfect condition as far as we can see. We thanked God for giving her to us on loan and we've offered her up to Him for His glory.

Excited and daunted
31 December 2007

We had reached the end of another year, so I wrote the following to encourage all our supporters:

"Expect great things from God. Attempt great things for God."

The man who wrote the above words described himself as "a plodder". If you want to see who he was, and what he managed to do with his life, then read on – it's quite an encouragement and a challenge. We can all do it!

I wonder how you feel as you enter this coming year? Excited? Daunted? Whatever word you might choose to use, God help us all to be faithful through both the highs and lows, the peaks and the troughs, of the coming year. "Excited" and "daunted" are both good words to describe how I feel. I'm excited because we have seen God's hand at work so massively thus far and anticipate more incredible times, and because it is such a privilege to serve the King of Kings. I'm daunted because we have such audacious plans and dreams for the transformation of Burundi which we can't do on our own, and because on a family level we've got vulnerable new baby Grace in Burundi, with its decidedly ropey medical facilities, along with the usual security, health, poverty and political issues.

I hope your own plans, dreams and aims for this coming year are not so modest that they are achievable in your own strength. That's what the above quote is about. That's what following Jesus is all about. Because He is the one "who is able to do immeasurably more than all we could ask or imagine" (Ephesians 3:20). Amen!

I realize more and more that wherever we are placed on planet earth, life is seldom straightforward and easy. In fact, it often seems to be downright messy, hard, dark and desperate. It's a battle. Maybe you're not struggling to find money for food, but you've got plenty of issues. Well, let's close with the example of the above "plodder" – not to feel condemned and inadequate, but to find a deeper resolve to embrace the challenge and adventure of being part of God's redemptive purposes for our lifetimes. It's not a dress rehearsal – let's do it!

Who was the plodder?

William Carey is often attributed the title "Father of Modern Missions". He was born into a desperately poor family and consequently obtained a terrible education. He was apprenticed as a shoemaker, but simply did not make the grade. He tried his hand at starting and running a school, but it functioned badly. His marriage was a deeply unhappy one, during which his daughter died early, an event which left him bald for life. He was a deeply committed believer, but his subsequent attempt at pastoring a small church hindered his chances of ordination because, by common consent, his sermons were too tedious and boring.

Despite such an apparently flawed track record, Carey formed a missionary society with himself as the first candidate setting sail to India. This feeble individual translated the Bible into Bengali, Oriya, Marathi, Hindi, Assamese and Sanskrit, as well as portions into twenty-nine other languages! At one stage, he lost ten years' translation work in a fire. What did he do? He just started again. Then there were contributions to literature, education, literacy, agriculture, getting infanticide outlawed, and more. This man's obedience and perseverance was used to impact the lives of literally millions of people. Before dying, knowing that others wanted to write about him, he wrote the following:

> If one should think it worth his while to write about my life, I will give you a criterion by which you may judge of its correctness. If he gives me credit for being a plodder, he will describe me justly. Anything beyond this will be too much. I can plod. I can persevere in any definite pursuit. To this I owe everything.

Whether anyone ends up writing about our lives or not, let us act out our dreams before the Audience of One with our respective God-given gifts, for His glory's sake. Happy plodding!

18

New Challenges

The Church exists for nothing else but to draw men into Christ,
to make them little Christs. If they are not doing that, all the
cathedrals, clergy, missions, sermons, even the Bible itself, are
simply a waste of time. God became Man for no other purpose.

C. S. Lewis

Welcome to PTI!
6 February 2008

Emmanuel Ndikumana and his wife Asele were the only
Burundians at our wedding and they prayed for us on
that day. He is probably the sharpest and most respected
church leader in the country. His pedigree is beyond
dispute. He was talent-spotted by respected theologian
and author John Stott, no less, and funded through
Allnations (we overlapped) for his theological degree and
then his Masters. Emmanuel is a deep thinker. He has been
overseeing international student work in the whole of
French-speaking Africa and has been outspoken at times
in Burundi, risking imprisonment or worse. Now it seems,

in God's timing, that he has embarked on something that will be highly impacting for this nation. The name of the organization is Partners Trust International (PTI).

Amazingly, Emmanuel's employers at IFES have recognized the hand of God in all this and have released one of their star men, which very few organizations would do, to follow his calling. It's hard to express his expansive vision succinctly, but essentially it involves three things: a church, a Bible school and a development organization, in that order, one flowing into the other.

There are very few churches in Burundi that I feel I really "fit" in. There are numerous reasons why. It might be because of language barriers, because of the preacher continually shouting and ranting, because it's plain dull, because the service is over four hours long, or because the teaching is shallow, heretical, or downright weird and I wouldn't want to take non-believers there. I think all that is about to change. Emmanuel's church will be (not exclusively, but predominantly) for the intellectuals – of which many are sat, totally dissatisfied and unstimulated, in the existing churches. More particularly, Bujumbura needs a church with a well-thought-through strategy, missiology and theology, with dynamic, bright, intellectually rigorous leadership and systematic Bible teaching. We expect people in due course to flock to this new church in droves – although, purposefully, the site chosen is slightly out of town in an area devoid of churches, so that no accusation can be raised of poaching people as a result of church-planting in the immediate vicinity.

It's hard to understand the dichotomy of the Burundian church. There are so many contradictions. It is growing so fast, but is utterly divided. It's a mile wide but an inch deep. There are many incredible men of God and many awful wolves in sheep's clothing. There are hardly (but with some notable exceptions) any church leaders who are esteemed by all as being men of true integrity. Good leadership models are almost non-existent. People start well but quickly get sucked into one of the three big temptations – money, sex and power – followed by an ensuing scandal.

The groups we as GLO work with are great, but notice that they are all interdenominational organizations. Yet, the church is ultimately God's chosen instrument and so we need some good models. I believe this new venture, with its accompanying Bible school, will provide that.

The perfect plot of land has been found with a sympathetic landlord. It's a massive plot, big enough to accommodate hundreds of cars as well as a big church building, and there is already a house on the plot which would serve as the Bible school. Until recently it was rented by the UN troops for $5,000 per month. Each step of this journey so far has been remarkable. The aim is to buy the property for $400,000 – a sum which Emmanuel and the landlord shook hands on, and we've been given a year to find the money. It will obviously have to be a "God-thing" for us to buy the land according to the agreed timescale, since it is a lot of money to find on top of our existing commitments. But I feel very passionate about the strategic import of this whole venture, and GLO will be in for the long haul. Recalling what SU was like ten years ago compared to what it is now is mind-blowing. I believe we will say the same thing a decade from now about PTI. Enough said for the moment.

Will you live out this dream with me?

God is allowing GLO to play a major role through our phenomenal local partners, and here is the next step. There is no better missiology than harnessing and empowering the best indigenous believers to transform their nation. This is the very heartbeat of GLO.

Progress at PTI
Monday 17 March 2008

The rollercoaster journey of starting up PTI is continuing apace. It is just six weeks since I first wrote introducing this exciting new venture, and God's hand is clearly leading the way. The owner of the land we are trying to buy is behaving in the most amazing way. He, Edward, is totally behind the vision without fully understanding it, to the extent that he has reduced the rent from the $5,000 per month which he was getting previously to just $1,750. Amazing! It turns out that he was supported through school by a Methodist missionary who wanted him to become a pastor, but Edward "went wrong" and chose business over God.

God now seems to be on his case and Edward is exhibiting extraordinary integrity. We have paid the rent up front for a year, with a verbal agreement to buy the plot before the year is up. Meanwhile (looking at this through the lens of spiritual warfare), as soon as we expressed an interest to use the land for the Lord's work, the World Bank showed up and said they wanted the plot, as did an Arab businessman, and then a top Rwandan trader. To put them off, Edward quoted them a price $200,000 more than the land's value. But they still want it! How many Christian businessmen would pass up on an extra $200,000 on a deal, based purely on their word of honor after a verbal commitment and a simple handshake rather than a contract? Although Edward is not yet a believer, he is getting closer and continues to tell us to keep praying!

Our agreement is to pay $400,000 for the land, but we now have just ten months left to raise those funds. Meanwhile, PTI visionary and founder Emmanuel is flying to the Ivory Coast to tender his resignation from his prestigious and secure job as head of training for Francophone African countries' student work. It is a bombshell to his team and there is wailing and tears, but as if in confirmation, just as he resigns, he gets an email from me informing him that a friend of mine has just contributed $100,000, a quarter of the needed sum. Hallelujah! Emmanuel kneels before his team and, amidst many tears, they pray him off with their blessing.

Some while later, in Ireland, I was handed 1.5 million Burundian francs ($1,500) in cash by our 98-year-old beloved supporter, Alison Hall, who I mentioned earlier. By this time the movement had been launched for a couple of months and was living pretty much hand to mouth. The new church had already outgrown its temporary venue and was having to meet outside the building. As a result, we researched the possibility of buying a big-top-style tent. A contact in Dubai reported back that they were prohibitively expensive and it all seemed somewhat discouraging and hard to resolve.

But Edward (still not a believer, but for whatever reason doing everything he could to help us) persuaded a friend of his in the tent-renting business to sell us some tents to meet in. At first the man refused, since he made his money from renting the tents, not selling them, but under pressure from Edward he relented. Then he found out it was for Emmanuel, who turned out to be a distant relative of his! He was willing to part with five tents, seating 200 people in total, and gave us an incredible price for them: just 300,000 francs each, a grand total of – you guessed it! – 1.5 million francs, the *exact amount* of money that has just come in from Ireland. It gives me goosebumps when this kind of thing happens!

There are two things that I am quite sure of:

1. This venture will succeed if we stay in God's will, listen clearly to what He is saying, and walk in close obedience to Him.

2. This venture will be hotly contested by the enemy all the way. It is no coincidence that the day PTI became

interested in the land and sought to purchase it, immediately big hitters like the World Bank showed up to muscle in on God's turf! Furthermore, some church leaders felt threatened by the model of integrated Bible-teaching and training at PTI, which is so sorely lacking in Burundi. There is the potential for misunderstanding and discord, then, even though the aim of PTI is to provide a model/resource of holistic, relevant, empowering training to the church in Burundi.

It is a constant challenge but I love this life of faith – embracing risks, taking on the impossible and acting out our dreams for the transformation of this land and beyond. It's clear to me that as we bless others, we get blessed. Emmanuel's salary with his former employers will soon come to an end, but he is stepping out in faith with his wife and three children. I'm behind him 100 per cent.

(Incidentally, in the end we didn't pursue the tent idea, but the land was duly bought for $400,000 and two substantial gifts totaling $320,000 came in immediately to put up a three-story building to accommodate students and provide further facilities.)

Tenacious heroes
20 March 2008

This morning I read about some truly authentic followers of Jesus – unnamed and unsung heroes of the persecuted church in North Korea, of whom plenty are now martyrs. Many believers (under probably the most oppressive regime in the world) recite daily the Lord's prayer and then the five principles of faith. Those principles highlight their expectations and understanding of the costliness of following Jesus:

1. Our persecution and suffering are our joy and honor.

2. We want to accept ridicule, scorn and disadvantages with joy in Jesus' name.

3. As Christians we want to wipe others' tears away and comfort the suffering.

4. We want to be ready to risk our lives because of our love for our neighbors, so that they also become Christians.

5. We want to live our lives according to the standards set in God's Word.

Wow! I don't envy their circumstances, but I do envy their authenticity!

I confess to frequently feeling like a fraud or an impostor. I aspire to being authentic in following my hero Jesus, but am I? We can talk a good game, but are we prepared to walk the walk? Of course, my context is totally different from the extremes of North Korea, but what is it costing me to say "yes" to Jesus' call, without conditions, caveats or compromises?

I have lots of lesser heroes out here who move me profoundly. There's Ahmed, who was a top Muslim and is now following Jesus at great cost to himself and his family. He's gone from being chauffeur-driven to facing death threats, having to flee, and is now sleeping under a car as he seeks to eke out a living for his loved ones as a night-guard. There's Jean-Marie who saw his parents' arms and legs hacked off as they bled to death. Yet he's forgiven the offenders and is totally passionate for all his countrymen, regardless of tribe, to experience the same love that God has poured out into his heart. There's Sarah, who visits in prison the man who wanted to rape and kill her and her kids and who, as a widow, has taken in several more orphans from the war without knowing how to support them all. I've listed just three heroes, but there are plenty more I could reel off.

The battle for Burundi continues to be waged. The ravages of war, poverty, HIV/AIDS and increasing Islamization are clear for all to see. This Tuesday I received an email about our YFC orphanage up-country. There was an armed robbery 300 yards away. One of our builders was killed and another couple of people are in a critical condition. People die for lack of food and medicine. There are plenty of discouragements to make God's people want to give up, but we know that the battle is the Lord's, so these heroic people I work and live with are more than just hanging in there for Jesus. Oswald Chambers said:

Tenacity is more than endurance, it is endurance combined with the absolute certainty that what we are looking for is going to transpire. Tenacity is more than hanging on, which may be but the weakness of being too afraid to fall. Tenacity is the supreme effort of a man refusing to believe that his hero is going to be conquered.

Amen!

Following Jesus, wherever we are, isn't a glamorous affair. We need to be clear about that. Jesus gave no soft sales pitch. Kierkegaard spells out the reality:

I long to accomplish a great and noble task, but it is my chief duty to accomplish humble tasks as though they were great and noble. The world is moved along, not only by the mighty shoves of its heroes, but also by the aggregate of the tiny pushes of each honest worker.

Spell I-S-L-A-M
18 April 2008

Last night saw the biggest attack on the capital for several years. Earlier in the day policemen were stationed on every street corner and rumors were flying around. Then at about 8.45 p.m. gunfire and shelling kicked off in a big way as the FNL rebels embarked on an audacious yet futile attack on various military installations about town. We had fourteen people in our lounge for home-group at the time. It is a surreal thing to listen to the big thuds of shells landing, the occasional whoosh of a rocket hurtling through the air and the rattling of machine gunfire, knowing that it is all real, that people are dying, maybe friends, certainly plenty of innocents caught in the crossfire.

This morning I rang various people to check they were OK. American friends across town had a gun-battle going on right next to them on the street. They shifted their three-year-old and newborn child onto the floor in the corridor, and the kids managed to sleep through the incredibly loud noises. Ours slept through as well, but it was all a bit further away from our part of town. Shadrach, who works for us, arrived early and immediately asked to be excused. Two of his children were missing, as they'd fled during the night and got separated. He's looking for them right now.

People expect there to be more attacks over the next few days. An aircraft flew overhead this morning to do some "mopping up" a few miles south of us. My colleagues are aiming to be back in their houses by 3 p.m. in case things flare up again. Hopefully this violent episode is just a blip, but the truth is that the economy is trashed, inflation is soaring, there have been fuel shortages and a recent substantial price hike, ordinary people struggle to afford to even eat, and with the alarming rate of population growth, there simply isn't enough land for everyone. Seen through human eyes, the outlook is bleak.

The death toll will be given in due course. However many it is, last night's attack highlights to me the urgency of our situation and our need to get people ready to meet their Maker. Bombs aren't raining down on the Western church, so I suspect many believers need a good kick up the backside to shake them from their complacency and re-evaluate their priorities. I know I do, and often! It's so easy to get distracted and caught up in things of little eternal significance. The battle is raging, but are we engaging?

Another manifestation of the battle for Burundi struck me again a few days ago when I was preaching in one of the areas hardest hit last night, just a couple of miles away. As I preached, the local Muslim evangelism team set up their loudspeakers and gathered a crowd. They held up the Bible and blasted out, full volume, all sorts of half-truths and distortions of its contents, which often seem very compelling to most nominal Christians without rigorous biblical foundations. They gave the microphone to a totally untrained representative of the Christian faith and trashed him before the crowd.

They have four such teams in the capital and each one goes out into the streets every Friday, Saturday and Sunday, with great success. It is difficult to counter them, as our work with Muslims who have converted to Christ shows: Islam is almost a one-way door. Those leaving Islam invariably get kicked out of their families and rendered destitute. That's a plain fact. I am not Islamophobic. For me, I-S-L-A-M stands for "I Sincerely Love All Muslims". But I can't believe how many people are taken in by their talk of it being a religion of peace. That's just choosing to ignore the facts. If proponents of Islam want to declare it a religion of peace, then let them define that peace more clearly, because it is peace on Islamic terms with non-Muslims paying a tax (*dhimmitude*) and not enjoying equal rights to Muslims. That is very clear in shariah law.

Talk of a religious war is premature, but only because, as yet, Muslims remain a very small percentage of the population. We support four evangelists who try to get along to those meetings, and they face very real danger as they stand up for the truth claims of Christ (indeed, one of the team was murdered last year in front of his wife and kids).

As the battle goes on in each of our different contexts, I'm challenged to consider that if my life is a lesson to others, what am I teaching them about how seriously I take my faith in God, how passionately I care about the fate of people around me, and how sacrificially I am willing to follow Jesus? It's a sobering thought.

19

CARING IN A WAY THAT COSTS

While women weep, as they do now, I'll fight. While little children go hungry, as they do now, I'll fight. While men go to prison, in and out, in and out, as they do now, I'll fight. While there is a drunkard left, while there is a poor lost girl upon the streets, while there remains one dark soul without the light of God, I'll fight – I'll fight to the very end!

William Booth

Modern-day Acts of the Apostles
8 October 2008

Do I love the truth enough to live it?

Get ready for some weird, wonderful and whacky stories of God at work in Burundi! Some stretch credibility, particularly for a Western mind, though an African wouldn't blink twice about them.

Onesphore has now reported back on the latest Harvest for Christ outreach from the summer. As usual, I am beautifully blown away by what happened. If I take a fresh look at the Acts of the Apostles in the Bible, I could almost substitute Burundi for "Antioch" or "Ephesus" and it would read in a similar vein. Here's a sample of what happened:

In Muyinga a prostitute called Victoria was kidnapped by cannibal witch doctors. They took a bite out of her thigh, but found that she tasted bitter, so the witch doctors didn't eat her (it sounds almost comical, except that it is true – one of the female members of our team asked to see some evidence to verify that she wasn't lying, and the mouth-shaped wound needed serious medical treatment). So instead the men cursed her and she became dumb. For three weeks she hadn't said a word when the evangelists arrived. She'd gone to the local administrator to press charges and he challenged the team: "If you want us to listen to you talk about your Jesus, then do something for this girl." They promptly gathered around her, prayed in Jesus' name, and Victoria began speaking again! The whole community was blown away by this obvious demonstration of God's power. The administrator promptly offered them land to build a church and, two months on, there is a church of a hundred members meeting there. Victoria is now a reformed ex-prostitute.

At Mukabira a powerful witch doctor was converted. On the spot he became an evangelist and invited the team to join him in addressing six other witch doctors. Those six duly gave their lives to Christ. They brought out all their charms, idols and spells, and had a public burning session, at which point the local craftsmen who had made the idols were in uproar (remember what happened in Ephesus in Acts 19?). They complained, "How dare these people come from outside and introduce strange ideas which take away our business?" They subsequently went to the local authorities and three of the team were arrested, beaten and held overnight.

In the morning, when it was established that they'd done

nothing wrong, they were released. As they stood outside the police station, still talking to several policemen, a tornado flared up. It is generally believed here that a tornado is an angry python underground sent by witch doctors. The policemen fled as the tornado approached, but the three believers stood their ground, at which point the tornado split into two, went around them, and demolished two houses on either side of them. The policemen then returned, totally awe-struck, asking, "Who are you people? What is your secret?" They replied, "The One who is in us is greater than the one who is in the world." More people were converted.

An example of Acts-style persecution involved a group being invited into a house on the pretext that they were being asked to share Christ. Once inside, however, they were beaten with sticks and a hoe. One young lad suffered serious head wounds and spent three days in hospital. Although they were the ones attacked, the evangelists were also the ones arrested. Onesphore drove there immediately and mediated. The aggressors begged forgiveness, and yet more people were touched by the power of God.

Vincent was steeped in witchcraft. He had made a pact with Satan and for twenty years hadn't been able to wear clothing, as it felt like pins were pricking him when it contacted his skin. He hadn't cut his hair in that time either and looked completely deranged. The whole area around Bubanza submitted to his spiritual leadership and lived in fear of him. He refused to listen to the team's first attempt to tell him about Jesus, but they persisted and returned. He was delivered, and when he burned all his charms, the community was so astonished that on the spot twenty other people gave their lives to Christ.

There are many more stories, but these are just a selection. Our God is a great big God! May He forgive us for keeping Him caged and domesticated.

Various radio stations broadcast multiple testimonies of the events, and the impact has been to stir and challenge the church to step up to the plate. Numbers aren't everything – and actually I don't want to over-emphasize the numbers, as reporting can sometimes be quite evang-*elastic*! But here is the top-line summary of what happened in just two weeks:

- 325 young people went out to share Christ in 26 of the least reached areas of Burundi.

- 46,917 people were spoken to one-on-one.

- 19,533 people were prayed with to receive Christ.

- 5,250 people were backslidden and recommitted themselves.

- 10 new churches were planted. Usually the idea was to work alongside a local church, but in some cases none existed.

- 74 witch doctors and 101 Muslims were converted.

- 15 marriages on the point of divorce were reconciled.

- 67 recorded healing miracles took place, including 5 paralytics walking, 3 blind people seeing, 8 demon-possessed people exorcised, and more.

I love being a part of this movement of fearless, passionate, sacrificial, bold, loving, Spirit-filled followers of Christ!

They challenge me in my own journey with Jesus. It's worth taking some time to reflect and pray through the following searching questions. Do those same words describe me too?

- *Fearless:* Am I liberated from or shackled by the fear of rejection, the unknown, the future, or the tyranny of public approval?

- *Passionate:* Do the gut-wrenching needs all around me move me to action, or do they make me adopt a resigned and dulled acceptance of the world as it is?

- *Sacrificial:* Am I embracing any cost in my walk with Jesus, or have I rationalized a more respectable and convenient cross?

- *Bold:* Am I a member of the fellowship of the unashamed, speaking the truth lovingly yet uncompromisingly in Jesus' name?

- *Loving:* Christ's love compels the teams in Burundi. As for me, do I really love people enough to share Christ with them in word and deed?

- *Spirit-filled:* Spiritually we "leak", so we need a daily, ongoing refilling with the Holy Spirit. Am I thirsty enough to take time to abide and drink deeply from the Fountain of Life and then to leak all over the people I meet?!

- *Follower of Jesus:* Am I His follower? Or do I expect Him to follow me on my terms and rubber-stamp whatever I choose to do with my life?

It was said of Dorothy Day that, "She loved the truth enough to live it." I find that incredibly stirring and it forces me to ask myself, "Do I love the truth enough to live it?" Taking things one stage further, I've been thinking about love and its opposite. You might think that the opposite of love is hate, but as followers of Jesus, I think the opposite of love is apathy. There is so much apathy in the body of Christ! My Burundian colleagues and friends don't display a shred of it. They love the truth enough to live it and they challenge me to do the same.

I realize that it is hard for most Western readers to relate to the above stories, but at the very least we can allow them to sharpen our prayers and help us understand, wherever we are in the world, that there is much more going on than meets the eye. The battle is real. Our enemy is real. The stakes are high and so prayer is crucial.

Clumsy but committed
8 October 2008

She lunges into my face with an open mouth, makes contact and pushes. Whether it's my nose she's latched onto or my cheekbone or my chin (or occasionally when she hits her intended target, my mouth!), she pushes hard and continues breathing through her nose. Grace is learning to kiss and it's a very wet process. Her efforts are clumsy but committed. She's nearly twelve months old. I'm her Daddy. I love her and I think she loves me!

There are worse things you could be called than "clumsy but committed". "Clumsy" may simply be a reflection of limitations, but "committed" reveals a positive heart attitude. I want to give God my best, indeed I am totally committed to that, but even my best efforts are clumsy in relation to His glorious perfection. But if, when I reach out to Him, He feels similar to how I feel when Grace slobbers on me, then I know He's just thrilled!

I'm no namby-pamby sentimentalist when talking about the love of God, don't worry, but I love that glimpse He's given me. His love cost Him a lot and was very raw. We are called to a similar costly and raw commitment.

Many coals in the fire
19 November 2008

I've just written to a friend I hadn't heard from for a while in response to his simple question: "What's happening with you?" This was my reply:

Where shall I start?

We have so much to be thankful for. Zac and Grace are generally very healthy. Lizzie continues to have the constitution of an ox with the beauty of a fat cow (a woman is referred to as a cow here in the marriage ceremony and fat is good, so that's a compliment!). I have recently recovered from a bout of dysentery and am now firing on all cylinders again. Health is not taken for granted here. Some German friends are evacuating today because of their sick baby and some American buddies were forced to leave for similar reasons last month.

Sat at my desk at dusk in humid Central Africa, I've just done a live breakfast radio interview for a station in freezing Canada – very surreal! The purpose of the interview was to talk about how God amazingly opened doors for us through a great brother called Bill Rice of YFC Edmonton, so that three containers that had just arrived from Canada could be released without any "charges" – something simply extraordinary here, as any dealings with customs usually involves bribery and corruption. But no bribes with us, no weeks of bargaining and pleading, and five new donated vehicles as well as many other things are now ours to use for God's glory. So many people around the world were praying. This saved us tens of thousands of dollars and we're all thrilled. Imagine the scene: as the containers were being unloaded we had ten volunteers trying to ward off a hundred customs officials who were prowling around, trying to steal anything when our backs were turned!

As I wrote the above paragraph, a colleague came in and asked for help. The heavy rains have washed away his roof and with five children, he has nowhere to shelter them. I have already helped him and this time I'll just pray. The fact is, he is the fiftieth person I've met this week, and indeed every week, who has urgent needs and who wants me to bail them out.

We can't help everyone financially, so we pray and ask God, meanwhile hoping to be strategic and discerning in what we get involved in – but it's hard.

Today on the news a six-year-old girl was found decapitated and without arms and legs. The reason? She was an albino. Albinos in Burundi are terrified right now, as they are being killed to satisfy the market for body parts that witch doctors in neighboring Tanzania use in their ritual magic.

At the moment we have visitors who are helping us get ready to launch by March what we hope will be the best conference center in Burundi. We are feeling overwhelmed at how complex it is and how much work has to be done in the coming months, but hopefully Goretti and Meg will recruit a fine team, get systems in place, and we will then not only be able to become self-sustaining but beyond that, profits will be recycled into God's work elsewhere around the country. I love that vision!

I have started a construction company with a gifted engineering friend called Emmanuel and that is going great guns – again, profits are fed back into our other projects and Emmanuel will, in due course, be able to build his own house with what he earns from it. Tomorrow Freddy (head of Youth for Christ) is moving into his very own house that GLO paid for him to build. Onesphore (head of Harvest for Christ) will move into his own house next month. This was part of my strategic vision to free up key leaders from worrying about providing for their family so they can concentrate on what God has given them to do.

Last Friday I wandered up the highest mountain in the centre of the country with a sharp knife, a goat and a lamb, to sacrifice them at the top. What happened on the peak? You'll have to wait to find out, as the film we are making is not yet ready. I have teamed up with a film-maker called Seth to make thirteen short films for a DVD to accompany each chapter of my book, *More Than Conquerors*. The June deadline is tight, but the four films produced so far are superb and I hope they will in due course be seen by many people and change many lives. For the rest of that weekend our SU team split up and spoke to fourteen school groups in order to equip them to shake the whole region. It was a great time.

Our building of the PTI Bible school is moving forward well and we have been involved in three other school-building projects. One is finished, one halfway and one not yet started.

Lots of visitors come and go. We have someone coming to stay with us tomorrow to do a week's intensive training in Evangelism Explosion, which is already living up to its name in terms of how many people are coming to Christ through this tool.

Before preaching this Sunday I will run down to the beach at 6 a.m. to meet with a team of passionate young evangelists and at 6.30 we will begin a new jogging club/outreach. There are several thousand joggers who meet there and, since they are jogging, they aren't going to church. We'll use a sketch to draw the crowds and then preach for just five minutes, then we'll go off running, come back, do the same sketch and preach to a new crowd, talk to people one-on-one, then come back next week and do the same. We are right at the start of this and I am both nervous and excited. I believe many will come to Christ in the coming months. I suspect Jesus would prefer to be jogging and hanging out with those guys than being sat in a pew – what do you think?

Our Muslim evangelism team is in as good a shape as it's ever been, slogging their guts out in dire poverty, facing very real threats of assault and murder, but willing to lay their lives down for the Truth. I find their example humbling.

A high-ranking official from Iran is here this week developing trade links. Iran follows Sudan and Libya as the key countries seeking to "help" Burundi. Can you spot what the conditions are? Beggars can't be choosers and Burundi is sadly forced to take help from wherever it can get it. Islam's growth is very concerning indeed.

Across the lake in the Congo things are just terrible. Some refugees have arrived here, although mostly it's further north from us. Systematic rape, murder and pillaging have taken place. It's all happening on our watch, but the international community simply doesn't have the will-power to intervene.

I can't really talk about politics if I want to carry on working here, but the challenges are massive and I really hope the recent arrest of a high-profile journalist-turned-politician isn't a sign of increasing repression and human-rights abuses as we approach the 2010 elections. Things are actually very unstable right now, with political stalemate and African Union troops about to pull out. They've helped keep the peace. When they go, what will happen? Serious prayer is needed.

Burundi lurches forward. The situation is superficially calm, but in reality it is grim for the vast majority and quite tense. Because I have been here for the last ten years I've now got a lot of potential influence, which to me is a mixture of humbling, terrifying and thrilling. Many people are trying to do bad things and I feel tired, yet so alive doing exactly what I think Jesus wants me to do. There is nothing like it. But it hurts and it's draining to care. As Jesus said, "From everyone who has been given much, much will be demanded" (Luke 12:48). I take that on the chin. It's a pleasure and a privilege to play a small part in His big plan.

That's a little of what's happening. You didn't expect such a long answer, did you?!

Oozing pus
11 December 2008

Christians have bumper stickers and catchphrases.
Believers have creeds and promises.
Disciples have scars and stories.

I'm feeling raw. I want to share that rawness with you. I apologize in advance for my jumble of thoughts and feelings, but please feel the anguish with me.

Today is my prayer day. There's a half-built Episcopal cathedral a hundred yards from my office so I often go there, take my shoes off, and stomp up and down praying in the cool and quiet. Today, after about an hour, a young lady interrupted me. Now you have to understand, I spend my life out here getting asked for money. It's relentless and draining to deal with. I thought to myself (whilst "in the Spirit") as she approached me, "Just go away, leave me alone, can't you see I'm praying? Don't you dare ask me for money!"

Her lips were quivering. She was dressed reasonably well, but she looked rough, with beads of perspiration on her nose. I could tell she was scared to approach me, but she was also clearly desperate, and desperation had triumphed over fear as she tentatively but boldly broke in on my special time with God.

Now hear me, I *am* compassionate. I feel people's pain. I do care, and I vote with my feet by going and giving, crying and caring. But still I thought, "Oh God, please, can't she just leave us alone together? I've had enough! Of course she's in need, but there are thousands of people in need. I can't give to everyone. Surely I can tell her to go away?"

"No, give her a chance. Just take a few minutes, listen to her story, give her some dignity."

So I did.

Sam told me she was feeling terrible. She'd just gone for an AIDS test to confirm the almost inevitable. She'd already been kicked out of her family and is four months pregnant by her boyfriend, who loves her but wants her to have an abortion. She talked of a wound she has that never heals and eventually showed it to me. It was disgusting! She peeled back her trouser-leg to reveal an oozing, pus-filled mess from above her ankle to below her knee. She could hardly walk. She'd had a motorbike accident the previous week, her back was sore, and she wanted to have an ultrasound scan to see if her baby was still alive.

Apart from feeling angry that my precious time with God had been interrupted, a number of other thoughts were going through my mind. While she spoke I was asking God if He wanted me to intervene. Or should I just pray for her? That's what I wanted to do, because then I could get back to my prayer time. But then I thought of one of my sermons last summer, which included the true story of a pastor who was too busy for a homeless lady who'd asked him to help her. He fobbed her off with a promise to pray for her instead. She wrote this poem and gave it to a local shelter officer:

I was hungry,
And you formed a humanities group to discuss my hunger.
I was imprisoned,
And you crept off quietly to your chapel and prayed for my release.
I was naked,
And in your mind you debated the morality of my appearance.
I was sick,
And you knelt and thanked God for your health.
I was homeless,
And you preached a sermon on the spiritual shelter of the love of God.

I was lonely,
And you left me alone to pray for me.
You seem so holy, so close to God,
But I am still very hungry – and lonely – and cold.

Ouch! So, Simon, are you going to practice what you preach?

"She's my daughter, in obvious pain, in a worse state than you've ever been, and all she's asking for is $10."

She carried on pouring out her woes. I carried on thinking as she spoke. "She's messed up. It's her own fault. She shouldn't have got herself pregnant. Why didn't she use a condom at the very least, especially if she has AIDS? That baby's going to be born into a hell of a life. How irresponsible! She's reaping what she sowed. I'm sorry, but we're all responsible for our actions."

"Let he who is without sin cast the first stone."

Did you stay chaste until you got married, or are you still a virgin, waiting to get married? If so, well done! I mean it. That's truly special. But for most of us, there's no way we can cast the first stone. I can't. All it takes is one time to get pregnant or to catch AIDS. It could have been me. It could have been you. But it's not, thank God. At least Sam wants to keep the baby, although she's being pressured to have an abortion. She's a victim in this – yes, she's guilty before a holy God, as we all are – but right now she needs love, dignity, and acceptance.

I asked if I could pray with her and shared the love and hope of Jesus. She didn't need to be told she was a sinner. She did need to know that it wasn't too late for her to turn. She decided to turn and repeated a prayer after me. Maybe it was just to please me. I hope not. God knows. That's between the two of them.

I gave her $10. I wanted to cry, but settled for a sad sigh.

Can we agree to pray about this?

For Sam, that when she comes back to see me tomorrow, she'll be able to tell me she's not got AIDS, that she's embracing a fresh start with Jesus, that her baby is still alive and kicking, and that her story will have a redemptive ending.

For me, that God would forgive my bad attitude, that my heart would remain soft, and that I'd be Jesus' hands and feet out here in Burundi, rather than just talking a good game.

For you – what should we pray? Be assured that however hard you have been squeezed by the credit crunch, things are not that bad. It's a question of perspective. I'm not belittling your problems, but Sam's certainly put mine into context.

We can't change the millions of Sams who exist, but we can all do our bit. Will you do your bit? Will you care in a way that costs you? Since God has made us in His image, have we gone and returned the favor? Maybe there's some serious repenting we need to do...

As Christmas approaches, it's not too late to choose to believe – maybe for the first time – in the radical incarnate message of Jesus, rather than being sucked into the consumerist lie; and not just to believe it's true, but to act out the truth of that belief. Not out of guilt, but out of gratitude. Whatever life throws at us, God cares enough to reach into the oozing pus of every situation. He did so much for me, I'm thrilled to be His. Sign me up! The Christmas story involves scars, not bumper stickers or slogans.

I said at the start I was feeling raw, so there's the raw challenge. It's your call. I'll pray for you as you pray for me.

Here's to Christmas scars, from the stable to the cross, or wherever our journey with Him leads us.

20

MINISTERING CHRIST TO "THE LEAST OF THESE"

Christ is the treasure chest in the field. And in him, I've found all that I'll ever need. No more trying to find purpose in ministry. No more looking for fulfillment in family or friends. No more needing to build something for God, or to be a success, or to feel useful. No more keeping up with the crowd, or trying to prove something. No more searching for ways to please people. No more trying to think or reason my way out of difficulties... I've found what I'm looking for!

David Wilkerson

Marijuana missionary
8 January 2009

I have a confession to make: I smoke marijuana each Sunday morning before going to church and I don't feel bad about it. In fact, it's my highlight of the week! More on this below...

At the beginning of this new year, I want to reflect on two questions:

1. What is God saying to you about your life for this year?
2. Will you follow Jesus wherever He leads you?

I don't in any way claim to have a hotline to God in terms of constant audible-voice experiences, but I do believe He is constantly speaking, if we'd only switch off the car radio/TV/iPod and get off Facebook/email long enough to really listen to Him. Silence is threatening to many of us, but surely that's when we're able to hear God's voice most clearly.

During the early part of last year, God spoke to me Sunday after Sunday as I drove to church and prompted me to begin the jogging/outreach ministry mentioned in the previous chapter. I would see thousands of people congregating on the beach and then jogging around together. If they were on the beach, then they weren't going to church and therefore weren't hearing about Jesus. It made me think that Jesus Himself would probably prefer to be there than in church, since He said He didn't come for the healthy but the sick. I decided to do both beach and church!

It took six months for me to respond to the regular nudges God was giving me and, after plenty of excuses – some lame, some legitimate – we began the jogging outreach. It's not very slick and polished, it's just fifteen passionate disciples of Jesus who want to meet people where they're at. We get laughed at, shouted at, scorned and slighted, but it's fine because Jesus is there and literally every week we introduce Him to new people! It's a beautiful sight to see people praying to receive Christ whilst footballs are flying overhead and crowds are jogging past. I leave the beach to jog home at 7.30 a.m., thrilled that people have caught the sweaty fragrance of Christ in our midst.

On the second Sunday of this outreach, after I had said my goodbyes and was heading home, I took a shortcut behind a shed and jogged past a few dozen youths smoking pot. I greeted them, they jeered at me, and I carried on past. But again, God spoke to me: "Go back and hang out with them. Church can wait. This is much more important." I carried on running, but then thought, "Simon, you may regret missing out on something special that God is lining up for you." I turned back and approached them.

"Hey, whitey, what do you want?"

I sat down on the ground with them. We got talking. Some were rude, some aggressive, most just intrigued. They handed me a joint. I hadn't smoked one since I was eighteen. As a servant of God, this was probably not the best idea. Hmm…

But every week since then I have loved jogging back home and stopping off to chat with the likes of Tigana, Abu and Fiston – young, misguided, messed-up men, who have so much potential for good or ill. They want to work, but there's no work to be had. It makes me wonder whether I too, in their position, would embrace their escapism as the best solution to the constant, suffocating blanket of despair which envelops them.

I could share a number of little vignettes with you from these times together. This Sunday just gone, one of the brash loudmouths took me aside from the rest of them. Claude had been incredibly rude and abusive to me a couple of weeks back, to the extent that even the others were embarrassed. He now appeared sheepish, but also determined to get something off his chest. "Simon, on TV last night they were talking about forgiveness and I thought of you. I realized when you come and talk to us, it's because you care, because you want to help us. I'm sorry for what I said to you." He looked me in the eye, smiled, shook my hand firmly and ran off.

By the time I get to church I'm exhausted! After all the running, my legs are heavy as lead, but my spirit is soaring. Jesus is definitely at church, but He's no less at the beach, and we've already had lots of time together.

Back to my two questions:

1. What is God saying to you about your life for this year?
2. Will you follow Jesus wherever He leads you?

Well...

... may we believe that God is constantly speaking to us throughout the coming year. May we tune out all competing sounds to listen intently to our glorious God who desires to communicate with us and take us on a great adventure. May we follow Jesus wherever He leads us – to the beach, the bar, the brothel or the bank. Anywhere. Everywhere. And may we be obedient to His call to embrace a messy, gritty, costly discipleship.

Let's do it!

P.S.: If you've caught the whiff of scandal from my comments about pot, then do now breathe a sigh of relief – it was only passive smoking!

Holy highs and lows
4 March 2009

We had seven days to find $80,000 to buy a crucial piece of land. Did we make it? Read on...

This week, I've experienced both highs and lows on my knees before the unfinished cement altar in what will soon be Bujumbura's new Episcopal Cathedral that I mentioned earlier. It's a stone's throw from my office and the place I go to pray, particularly on Wednesdays, my prayer day. I love it there. A half-built church resonates with me: it speaks of work in progress, a long way to go, messy but constantly evolving and hopefully becoming steadily more beautiful.

Over the last few months the builders have gotten used to me showing up, taking my shoes and socks off and stomping up and down, either singing on the guitar or seemingly muttering to myself. Then one day I asked permission from the foreman to share something with them all as a group. He agreed. So one lunchtime, as they munched away during their break, I took the opportunity to tell them about the Master Builder.

I told them what a privilege they had to build such a temple for God to dwell in. But did they know the One they were building it for? If they didn't, the incredible news was that they could. Of the fourteen there, one of them had the courage to raise his hand to accept the invitation. Four of them came back to my office to get Bible-reading notes. Then the following week, whilst I was praying again, another one of them sidled up to me, genuinely convicted, and wanted to surrender to Christ. Holy highs indeed!

Back to this week: On Monday and Tuesday I was there, on my knees, feeling discouraged and low, and pleading with God for Him to give us the strategic additional plot of land next to SU's conference center. It would be an excellent asset and would help us, in due course, to multiply profits to sow back into kingdom work in Burundi. Surely, He wouldn't let us miss this opportunity? We'd been given a week to find $80,000 and after three days only $10,000 had come in. That's when I shared the burden with our supporting network.

The response was astounding. So many people have made contributions, large and small, over the last few days. I am delighted to say (and have been on my knees in gratitude today at that unfinished altar) that we have got way more than the required amount for the land, and with a day to spare! I feel as high as a kite. We've contacted the owner and will sign for it when he returns from a trip abroad. About $250,000 came in and all that money is fantastic provision, because so much needs doing to the land anyway.

Then, just a few minutes ago, there was a knock at my office door and in walked Sam. I'd not seen her since that day, just under three months ago, when our encounter in the unfinished cathedral broke my heart. I'd prayed for her ever since and subsequently kicked myself for not doing more for her at the time. It was another holy moment. Her leg is still oozing pus. She's now eight months pregnant and through lack of food is likely to have a premature birth. I'd prayed for her to receive Christ and I'd wondered if she was just doing it for me, but here she was, telling me she'd just come from praying at church.

A high.

She smiled a pained smile.

I had to ask her.

"So, was your AIDS test positive or negative?"

It's such a blunt question. You know that in the next breath you'll find out whether this person in front of you will be dead in the next few years or not.

"Positive…" (Pause.) "That's life. I'm on anti-retrovirals, so hopefully baby will be fine."

A low.

Why did you send her today, Lord?

I was just getting a prayer letter ready. I think He wanted people to know.

Holy highs and lows in Burundi. That's life…

Thank you for sharing this incredible, raw, rollercoaster adventure in Burundi with us. Thank you for lightening our load. Thank you for encouraging and loving and praying and giving. If you, like me, resonate with the image of a half-built church, if you recognize you're a work in progress with a long way to go, then enjoy loving and living for the God of big, strategic land acquisitions, but also small, seemingly insignificant lives. He is our Emmanuel through both highs and lows, wherever we are.

The least of these
24 March 2009

I've just seen Sam again. Two weeks ago she showed up, eight months pregnant, and confirmed the worst news – that she was HIV positive. The following Sunday, our baby Grace was very sick, so I stayed at home to look after her. It was the only Sunday in many months that I was at home and I think it was providential as Sam rang. She'd been hit by a car and had given birth to a dead baby. She wouldn't be released from hospital unless she paid her bills, which needed paying immediately (unpaid bills here means imprisonment). I was able to help her to get out of hospital and avoid jail.

Sam, twenty-eight years old, is at the bottom of the world's pile. Her system is slowly shutting down. Her leg is still oozing pus. She has nobody in the world to look out for her. And she came back to see me just now.

She is "one of the least of these" that Jesus spoke about (Matthew 25). What I do for her, Jesus says I'm doing for Him. Somehow she is Jesus for me today. What should I do with this Jesus sat in front of me? She's in pain. Her leg wound stinks. Her bleeding, post-miscarriage, is continuing. Her hands are trembling. She picks nervously and aggressively at her long, grimy fingernails.

"Simon, can I ask you something?"

"Go ahead."

"I don't want to beg. I want to work. I need to earn enough money for food and medicine. Can you give me enough to start a business?"

I'm so glad she's not begging, that she has the will to work, that she still has some form of bent hope.

"How much do you need?"

"$100 is enough to buy a phone and some units to sell to people who can't afford their own phone."

I'm aching inside. I'm challenged. You see, I'm all about the big picture and strategic involvement. Sam, however, is very small picture and not strategic at all. To be blunt, she'll probably be dead in the next few years.

But God doesn't see her that way.

So neither can I.

I give her $110, the bit extra to treat her leg wound. I squeeze her, in an attempt to show her some real, pure, non-sexual, fatherly love. As soon as she walks out of my office, three of my colleagues run up to me and warn me about her. She's a thief! She's a loose woman! She's a liar! Angry tears well in my eyes. Come on, guys! She may have been all three of those things, but she also bears the imprint of Christ! And hopefully she's changing. She's definitely not lying about her repulsive, stinking wound, her HIV status, her lost baby. She's messed up – that's as clear as can be – but please, who are we to judge? First take the plank out of your own eye and deal with your own Pharisaic yeast infection!

Although I'm angry, I realize that my judgmental anger towards them risks worsening my own Pharisaic yeast infection.

Did Jesus come to you today, in whatever guise? I think He did. I think He does, every day, sometimes very "inconveniently". And when He came, what did you do? What did you say? If you didn't recognize Him, don't worry, He'll be back. Next time you can choose to be ready.

When He comes, what should we do? Jesus tells us what He will say to us one day, those awe-full words in Matthew 25: "Whatever you did (not do) for one of the least of these, you did (not do) for me."

Thank you, Lord, for sending Sam into my life to challenge my selfishness, my busyness, my hard heart and my abstract theology. May God help us to…

… see Jesus in others

… and be Jesus to others.

From dream to reality
22 May 2009

Today we formally opened the King's Conference Center. It went well, with lots of dignitaries and guests in attendance. I was happy to have Mum and Dad here to share the day and only a little disappointed that the President couldn't make it. Now the challenge really begins (as I said in my speech) to make it the best in Burundi, by modeling excellence in Jesus' name. Then all the profits made can be ploughed back into SU's fantastic ministry country-wide, and thus they will no longer need outside funding. That is the aim. Self-sustainability is so hard in such a broken economy, but I hope we'll crack it. In the last few months, the KCC has been operating and has already acquired a good reputation, but now things will become much more high profile. Indeed, we were on national television this evening.

The whole experience of building this monster has absolutely knocked the stuffing out of me. I've had enough. From going to India to order furniture (not my skill set at all) to contending with officialdom for customs clearance, to shoddy workmanship on occasion, miscommunication, financial stress, seeking to build a high-quality staff team, the lot. I have made mistakes and someone else could have done a much better job than me. Yet the dream has become a reality and I hope that one of my mantras will thereby be fulfilled: "a missionary's job is to do himself out of a job". The KCC is my ticket to redundancy at SU, so long as it generates sufficient funds, and that'll mean I can go and have a quiet life elsewhere! Well, there is no room for self-congratulation or resting on our laurels. We now have to prove ourselves and bring glory to our King, after whom the center is named.

C.O.M.E.

14 June 2009

Oswald Chambers wrote:

> If you abandon everything to Jesus and come when He says,
> "Come," then He will continue to say, "Come," through you.
> You will go out into the world reproducing the echo of Christ's
> "Come". That is the result in every soul who has abandoned all
> and come to Jesus. Have I come to Him? Will I come now?

I've just preached my last sermon in Burundi for a while. I'm packing up and leaving. This leg of the journey is over and, at least for a season we'll be elsewhere, but Burundi still beats in my blood!

I'm not prone to nostalgia or excessive introspection, but my sermon on Abram's call allowed me briefly to look back at the incredible joy of living dangerously for Jesus in this precious land. It's just over a decade ago that I arrived, having left everything I knew behind. With a backdrop of constant shooting and shelling, and only a few hundred dollars in the world, I was believing and acting on what God said to Abram: "Leave (everything) and go (where) I will show you." True to his Word, He showed me.

Entering such a war zone and taking such risks, I never thought I'd reach the age of thirty, let alone have the chance to get married and make babies. Friends died around me. I nearly died – many times. If I had, I guess I'd be celebrating right now, having a whole lot more fun than even this "life to the full" that I am currently enjoying.

What was the biggest lesson I learnt?

Everything is a gift. My roaring, untamed, Savior Jesus; my faithful, fun and feisty wife Lizzie; my gorgeous two-and-a-half children, Zac, Grace and No. 3, due at the end of July; our supportive families and friends; Burundian brothers and sisters who raise the bar to what is possible if we embrace a costly cross; freedom to be who we are created to be; health, daily bread, education; the prayers and financial support of fellow Christians; hope – both now and eternal. The list goes on! But I encourage you to take stock right now, because grateful people make happy people. Most of us spend way too much time moaning about how hard our lot in life is.

The Lord continues to do incredible things in Burundi and it's such a privilege and joy to be a part of. He has truly done "immeasurably more than all [I could] ask or imagine" (Ephesians 3:20) over the last decade, and long may it continue. It blows my mind to review what has happened – the fact that we are now living in peace, however fragile it is – and all the glory goes to Him.

Olivia Perry-Smith is taking over GLO's in-country operations management whilst my family and I move to the USA for a few years. Why there? In brief, it's to preach around America, to stir up more radical disciples, and also to network and mobilize prayer and resources for kingdom work in Burundi.

Back to this morning's sermon. It was entitled "The Adventure of Calling", and if you want to experience it, like Abram, you have to C-O-M-E:

Claim God's promises
Obey God's instructions
Maintain faith in God's leading
Embrace risks for God's glory

So, if you COME to Jesus, abandoning everything for His sake, "He will continue to say 'Come' through you" and "you will go out into the world reproducing the echo of Christ's 'Come'. That is the result in every soul who has abandoned all and come to Jesus. Have I come to Him? Will I come now?"

Here's to reproducing that echo!

EPILOGUE

So much more could have been included in these pages, but I wanted to give you glimpses of what the Lord has done through some phenomenal brothers and sisters of faith, as well as through fickle me. I've shared some deeply personal issues and chosen not to gloss over my weaknesses. We often put people on a pedestal, which doesn't do them any favors. I know my own heart, which makes it all the more incredible to me to see how the Lord has poured out His grace in my life and allowed this wavering servant of His the opportunity to enjoy such an amazing, fruitful, painful and exciting journey.

The last ten years have been remarkable. I wonder what the next decade will look like for Burundi, which is always seemingly on the verge of imploding. Since we left Burundi, Josiah Monty has arrived on the scene and joined the Guillebaud team (Lizzie went into labor whilst I was making an altar call at a youth meeting a couple of hours away, and I was glad to make it back in time!). We love him dearly and are pretty confident that he'll be the last, but not least, in our quiver! The plan, which is always provisional and could change at any moment as the Lord leads, is to return to Africa after a couple of years in the States.

Meantime the King's Conference Center has gone from strength to strength and employs over fifty people. Olivia

Perry-Smith and Goretti Wege have helped turn it into the best conference center in Burundi. The President's wife comes three times a week with four jeeps' worth of bodyguards to use the gym(!), the World Bank and the UN, along with many NGOs, are enjoying our services, and it is fulfilling its stated aim to provide excellence in Jesus' name to bring glory to the King, whilst generating very significant profits ($16,000 last month) to plough back into God's work and helping Scripture Union attain self-sustainability. That is thrilling and very encouraging to me.

Scripture Union continues to train ever-increasing numbers of students, pastors and churches in evangelism and discipleship country-wide. The Aid for AIDS project has pioneered a Christian approach in the nation to the pandemic. Youth camps are run to equip and mobilize the leadership of school Christian groups to be effective where they are. The *Jesus* film is shown annually to tens of thousands of people with very significant fruit. We have opened and are operating out of a further two regional offices and have built a school in the North in partnership with Fields of Life, who have also helped three of our other partners.

At Youth for Christ, Freddy is concentrating on raising a new generation of leaders of high caliber. The Future Hope orphanage is a beacon of light and an oasis of life and joy, and the children are being trained very intentionally to become future leaders in the nation. It's a twenty-year vision. The school and medical center service the community and Freddy's ambitious plans and further involvement include houses for widows, a vocational training facility and another school.

Onesphore continues to encourage me at every turn. One of his many goals is to have an evangelistic team on every hill in the country by 2020, which doesn't seem realistic until you realize that he has over-delivered on all the expansion targets he has set his team at Harvest for Christ so far – truly remarkable. His peace groups on different university campuses have been trained and prepared to defuse volatile situations and stop bloodshed occurring, which historically always took place when the political situation was at crisis point. His vision for Burundi to be a sending nation to North Africa is coming into being, with missionaries in training already as they work in the bush with the pygmies (the Batwa). More and more breakthroughs are being made with the resistant Twa as they see real love in action through Harvest for Christ's involvement – literacy assistance, a school, farming training, clothes distributions, advocacy for land rights, etc. I can't resist including his latest email about the work. It reads:

> Manariyo used to work as a representative of the Batwa at Busiga. He was repeatedly let down by many NGOs who promised much but delivered nothing. When we went to work in Busiga he didn't want to be identified as the Batwa community leader. His heart was wounded. Six months later, Passy [who is our HFC lady working with the Batwa there] saw him coming to church. He decided to give his life to Christ. And when Passy asked him why, he brought all the agreements that NGOs had signed with him which hadn't been respected and said, "Since you have come here, I carefully observed you. I discovered love that I have not seen in any other persons who visited us. I am sure that you are people of God and you love us Batwa. I decided to give my life to the Lord you serve and who pushed you to come to us." Manariyo is a new convert and Passy is discipling him. His wife also started coming to church. God is slowly opening the hearts of the normally very resistant Batwa.

Evangelism Explosion as a tool is simply incredibly effective in Burundi. Onesphore built it up and then handed on to Leon, who is likewise a zealous strategic thinker and has further grown the work. Churches are lining up to benefit from the training and seeing their congregations swell as the laity get mobilized and equipped to reach out into their communities. Leon is the man who started the jogging outreach with me on the beach and has driven it forward, and I love the fact that week by week people come to know Jesus down there amidst the crowds of sweaty bodies.

Partners Trust International is growing faster than we can handle. Its founder and leader Emmanuel is extremely stretched. The needs are huge. Heads of denominations are coming to him and asking, "Will you train all our people?" because they recognize him as a man of integrity, intellectual capacity and strategic vision. Whereas elsewhere, Western programs are imported and imposed without much or any contextualization, Emmanuel and his team know what the church really needs and are addressing the key issues. Pastors are coming to be trained and then sent back to their denominations with a much more rounded and healthy approach to ministry, recognizing that they need to do things very differently to how they had been taught. I am totally convinced that PTI will be the most key vehicle for the healthy shaping and equipping of the church in Burundi, as it aims not to be a denomination, but rather to serve and resource other denominations in terms of modeling expository preaching, children's work and holistic development.

Outreach on campuses through UGBB (Union des Groupes Bibliques de Burundi) and equipping of university students is taking place, although we'd love to do so much more in this area. Funding remains a big challenge. And our Muslim evangelism team, APRID, having survived a number of tricky episodes, is hopefully now operating on a more even keel, although again for lack of funding the challenges and needs are simply huge, with the onslaught of well-funded and trained Muslim groups penetrating the interior and spreading Islam at an alarming rate.

The More Than Conquerors book and DVD (with thirteen films on it) are being circulated and used around the world, and are having a positive impact in stirring up individuals and groups to radical discipleship. Do check them out at www.more-than-conquerors.com and get them if you haven't yet.

So we are engaged at multiple, strategic levels in trying to contribute to the strengthening of the body of Christ in Burundi. It's a wonderful privilege to be involved. I want to make clear too, that there are plenty of other groups doing great things, so don't get the impression that it's all about what we're doing. The emphasis of this book has been on GLO's partners' activities, but there are many others seeking to help serve Burundi and her people in Jesus' name.

The needs are often overwhelming and the challenges are certainly huge, but God is sovereign, He is faithful, and we trust in Him to see that nation transformed for Jesus' sake. There is absolutely no room for complacency or self-congratulation. The battle is raging. So here's a question:

Do you want to join our team? I'd love you to. This is a direct invitation to get involved. Please do. How?

Firstly, pray. Prayer has been and will always remain the bedrock of our work – and how the Lord has honored the prayers of the tens of thousands who are behind us! Do pray for us. Just email info@greatlakesoutreach.org and ask to be kept up to date.

Secondly, contribute financially to the work. A little money goes a very long way out in Africa. A monthly amount, or a one-off gift, would be a huge blessing. Again, please contact us.

Thirdly, why not come out and see for yourself, and check out whether what I've written is true? You could volunteer for anything, from a few weeks to a few months, and help where there is need – and there is always plenty of need!

So do get in touch, please, to get our prayer news, or to give, or to enquire about visiting, by emailing info@greatlakesoutreach.org or checking out www.greatlakesoutreach.org

The prayer that took me out to Burundi in 1998 was, "God, I'll do anything, I'll go anywhere. Just make it clear." I could never have imagined what that would result in. The Lord has surpassed my wildest dreams. I hope you will choose to echo that prayer and maybe I'll get to see you out there some time. But whether our paths cross or not, here or there, I hope this book has stirred your heart to give your life unreservedly to the Lord Jesus Christ. Don't hold back. Don't settle for less than the best.

Please choose to be dangerously alive!

Simon Guillebaud
February 2011

ACKNOWLEDGMENTS

Tim Pettingale, for sorting through a messy first draft, editing, reordering, and generally making this book hopefully a more coherent and gripping read.

All those thousands of faithful folk who pray for us. I am astounded and humbled at how many people come up to me at conferences or in churches and say that they pray for us every day. To each and every one of you, I always say the same: "I am *so grateful* to you. As you've seen, your prayers have been abundantly answered. God bless you so much!"

Mark and Charlotte Hutchinson, quality buddies, for reading through the manuscript and making a lot of helpful suggestions/recommendations.

Ed Walker, for the kind words in the foreword and the laughs we've shared over the years.

Steve and Hilda White, both for GLO involvement and for being superb hosts for lots of fun weekends.

Tim Grew at the BBQ! And then all that led to, through Mark Bailey, Mark Melluish and the New Wine Network. I'm very grateful for all you guys' support.

Jill Ford and Allnations in Hertfordshire, for allowing us to be a part of a special community at a tricky time.

Matt Klein, for getting involved with us and sharpening our communication to the outside world.

In memory of Pat Symons, and thanks to Cheryl Law and Shawn DuPre and the GLO Boards in both the USA and the UK, for the crucial work you are involved in back home which enables us to have such a beautiful impact on the field.

Rob de Berry, whose obedience in the first place to God's prompting set me off on this crazy journey.

Inspiring visionary leaders Freddy Tuyizere, Onesphore Manirakiza, and Emmanuel Ndikumana, for your friendship, for modeling the real deal, and for encouraging me to dream big and not settle for less than the best.

All the staff at Scripture Union Burundi, for giving me the privilege of being on your team, which has involved countless extreme scenarios, hilarious moments, and fruitful times.

Seth Chase, for spicing up two years in Burundi with our filming escapades – getting stopped by police, mugged by street kids, and a whole lot more. And I believe that the end product, the *More Than Conquerors* DVD series, has already had and will have progressively a bigger impact than we both could have imagined. I'm indebted to you, so thanks a lot for the adventures.

Olivia Perry-Smith, for surpassing my already high expectations as GLO National Director in Burundi.

Mark Harris, Trey and Emily Mamo, Dave Souter, Bill Rice, Andy Clarke, Phil Hadley, Mary Page Carmody, Mike Breen, Paul Smith, and Trevor Stephenson, for your generosity and/or strategic involvement in GLO's work, such that things are moving forward faster and better than I honestly hoped or expected. And thanks to all those who have sown financially into our work over the years.

To Steve Wood, Kurtz Smith, and all our current community at St Andrew's, who have embraced us with such generosity.

Mum and Dad Guillebaud, truly fabulous parents, and Dum and Mad Corfe, equally fabulous in-laws, for your unstinting and selfless support and endorsement – such a gift.

Lizzie – my best mate, my love mate, my life mate. It's not easy to be married to me, and you manage it so well! I know it's much harder for you when I'm often away and you're doing the less glamorous but crucial work of looking after Zac, Grace and Josiah. You're a fabulous mother. You know I appreciate you, value you, and love you so much. Thanks for saying yes.

GREAT LAKES OUTREACH

A few years ago, I set up Great Lakes Outreach (GLO), which works in partnership with several organisations in the Great Lakes region of Central Africa, notably in Burundi. Its purpose is to respond to the area's massive needs and the huge potential impact of strategic involvement in cooperation with key Burundian partners.

The main areas of GLO's involvement include:

- Evangelism and discipleship through schools and churches
- Printing of teaching materials
- Fighting the AIDS pandemic
- Helping to sustain an orphanage
- Equipping and encouraging informed dialogue between Christians and Muslims
- Training university students in outreach
- Small business development opportunities to enable income-generation and self-sustainability

All proceeds from the sale of this book will go to the work of GLO. I would love you to get involved in what the Lord is doing out in Burundi, so do get in touch by contacting info@greatlakesoutreach.org or visit our website: www. greatlakesoutreach.org There are opportunities to come out on short-term teams, to contribute financially, to become a regional representative, and to subscribe for more detailed and personal prayer information. I look forward to hearing from you.